PENGUIN CLASSICS

A SHORT ACCOUNT OF THE
DESTRUCTION OF THE INDIES

BARTOLOMÉ DE LAS CASAS was born in Seville in 1484. At the age of eighteen he left Spain for the New World, where he participated in the conquest of Cuba and witnessed the first full-scale massacre of an Indian community. He became a priest and, after a 'conversion', entered the Dominican order. Thereafter he dedicated himself to the protection and defence of the Indians. After witnessing the ravages and atrocities of the Spanish colonists and the tragic failure of his own project for a peaceful colony in Cumaná, he wrote the *Short Account of the Destruction of the Indies* in 1542. The book was dedicated to Philip II and was, Las Casas claimed, intended to inform the Spanish crown of what was happening in America, as a warning that if the actrocities continued God would destroy Spain as a punishment. This astonishing work – a fierce, informed, deeply atmospheric anatomy of genocide – was immediately translated into every major European language and for three hundred years established the image of the Spanish conquest of America in the eyes of Europe. Las Casas wrote innumerable other works in defence of the Indies, including one of the earliest studies in comparative anthropology (*The Apologetic History of the Indies*) and a general *History of the Indies*. He died in 1576.

ANTHONY PAGDEN is Professor of History and Political Science at the University of California, Los Angeles. He has written widely on the history of Europe's relationship with the non-European world, and on the history of imperialism, ancient and modern. His books include *European Encounters with the New World*, *Lords of all the World*, *Ideologies of Empire in Spain, Britain and France* and, most recently, *Peoples and Empires*.

NIGEL GRIFFIN read Modern Languages at Oxford, taught there and at the University of Manchester, and has held visiting professorships in Italy and Hungary. He is the author and editor of several books and monographs on early modern Spanish and Portuguese literature and history and now works as a freelance translator and editor. His publications include *Las Casas on Columbus*.

BARTOLOMÉ DE LAS CASAS

A Short Account of the Destruction of the Indies

Edited and Translated by NIGEL GRIFFIN
With an Introduction by ANTHONY PAGDEN

PENGUIN BOOKS

PENGUIN BOOKS

Published by the Penguin Group
Penguin Books Ltd, 80 Strand, London WC2R ORL, England
Penguin Group (USA), Inc., 375 Hudson Street, New York, New York 10014, USA
Penguin Books Australia Ltd, 250 Camberwell Road, Camberwell, Victoria 3124, Australia
Penguin Books Canada Ltd, 10 Alcorn Avenue, Toronto, Ontario, Canada M4V 3B2
Penguin Books India (P) Ltd, 11 Community Centre, Panchsheel Park, New Delhi – 110 017, India
Penguin Books (NZ) Ltd, Cnr Rosedale and Airborne Roads, Albany, Auckland, New Zealand
Penguin Books (South Africa) (Pty) Ltd, 24 Sturdee Avenue, Rosebank 2196, South Africa

Penguin Books Ltd, Registered Offices: 80 Strand, London WC2R ORL, England

www.penguin.com

First published 1992
Reprinted with a Chronology and Further Reading 2004

046

Filmset in 10½/13 pt Monophoto Garamond

Printed and bound in Great Britain by Clays Ltd, Elcograf S.p.A.

ISBN-13: 978-0-140-44562-6

www.greenpenguin.co.uk

Penguin Books is committed to a sustainable
future for our business, our readers and our planet.
This book is made from Forest Stewardship
Council™ certified paper.

CONTENTS

A SHORT ACCOUNT OF THE DESTRUCTION
OF THE INDIES

Illustrations appearing on pages 16, 47, 49, 59, 62, 73, 112 and 118 are by the Flemish engraver Theodor de Bry and are taken from a sixteenth-century Dutch edition of the *Short Account of the Destruction of the Indies*. They are reproduced by kind permission of the British Library.

For Harriet and Felix

ACKNOWLEDGEMENTS

The editor would like to thank Dr A. Gordon Kinder of the University of Manchester and Dr Clive Griffin of Trinity College, Oxford, both of whom read the text of the translation and made helpful suggestions.

Previous page: Map of America (Basle, 1540) showing the standards of Spain and Portugal.

INTRODUCTION

I

The *Short Account of the Destruction of the Indies* was the first and the most bitter protest against the excesses of European colonization in the Americas, and its author, Bartolomé de Las Casas, 'Defender and Apostle to the Indians', the most controversial figure in the long and troubled history of Spain's American empire. In the four hundred years since his death he has been given many roles to play: the voice of a European Christian conscience raised against the casual slaughter of thousands of 'barbarians' in a remote, barely imaginable quarter of the globe; the creator of the 'Black Legend', a distorted Protestant-inspired record of Spanish atrocities and cruelties which was to darken every attempt to exonerate Spanish imperial ventures from the sixteenth to the eighteenth centuries; the distant, unwitting father of Spanish-American independence, 'that friend of humanity', in the words of 'The Liberator' Simón Bolívar, 'who with such fervour and determination denounced to his government and his contemporaries the most horrific acts of that sanguineous frenzy'; and the equally unwitting progenitor of today's Liberation Theology. In Latin America he is still ubiquitous. Even in Spain, despite murmurings of protest from the Catholic reactionaries of the late nineteenth century, he has been hailed as the 'authentic expression of the true Spanish conscience', in an attempt to explain away the destruction of the 'Indian' peoples as a passing aberration in the nation's history. And for many, both in Spain and beyond, his presence seems, somehow, to redeem the inescapable complicity of all Europe in the Spanish conquests. The Abbé Guillaume Raynal, author, together with Diderot, of the *Philosophical and Political History of the Two Indies*, the fiercest and the most widely read condemnation of European colonialism to be written during the Enlightenment, looked forward to a more generous age when 'these unfortunate lands which have been destroyed will be repopulated and acquire laws, customs, justice and liberty'. And he imagined a statue of Las Casas, 'in which you will be shown standing between the American and the Spaniard, holding out your breast to the dagger of the latter to save the life of the former. And on the base such words as these should be inscribed: IN A CENTURY OF FEROCITY, LAS CASAS, WHOM YOU SEE BEFORE YOU, WAS A BENEVOLENT MAN'. There are now, throughout the Americas, dozens of such statues.

Some of Las Casas's many identities have been devised to serve political and moral interests he would not have shared and may not even have understood. The 'Black Legend' was largely an instrument of Anglo-Dutch propaganda, and he would have been horrified at the uses to which the despised Protestant heretics had put his work. Independence from Spain was something he never contemplated even for the Indians, let alone the descendants of the conquistadores themselves. Liberation Theology's implicit claim that the 'poor of Christ' possess a privileged understanding of the human condition comes close to his self-consciously prophetic, apostolic vision of the new American Church. Nevertheless, he would never have accepted any kind of revolt against the power of either the Church or the State. His attacks on the behaviour of the conquistadores, on the agents of the Crown, even on members of the clergy were relentless and uncompromising. But he was never once during his lifetime formally accused of heterodoxy, nor ever suspected of treason. Only his fiercest enemy, Juan Ginés de Sepúlveda (to whom I shall return) suggested that his writings were heretical and a threat to the interests of the Spanish monarchy. Las Casas, in fact, regarded all rebels as disrupters of 'the common reason of man'. Like many radicals, he was, in all respects but one, the staunchest of conservatives. Self-educated, his massive if erratic learning was directed only against those who argued that the conquest of America had conferred upon the Castilian Crown rights to the goods or the labour of the native inhabitants of the Americas.

Las Casas's understanding of the historical and eschatological significance of the discovery and conquest of America contrasted an early vision of peaceful settlement with the rapacious horrors of the conquests which followed. Columbus, whose diary he preserved and edited, had, in Las Casas's view, been chosen by God for his learning and virtue to bring the Gospel to the New World. It was for this, he wrote, 'that he was called Christopher, that is to say *Christum ferens*, which means carrier or bearer of Christ'. It was the Spanish settlers, men precisely like Las Casas as he had once been, who had transformed a trading and evangelizing mission not unlike that practised by the Portuguese along the coast of Malacca into genocidal colonization. Twice, once in Cumaná on the Venezuelan coast between 1520 and 1521, and then again between 1545 and 1560, in the optimistically named Verapaz ('True Peace'), a region in modern Honduras, Las Casas attempted to create peaceful settlements of the kind which the missionaries might have been able to build if the Spanish colonists had not got there first: settlements of priests and honest farmers. Both experiments failed. The priests at Cumaná and the 'simple labourers' whom Las Casas had fetched from Castile for the purpose were massacred after a slaving raid on the area by Guayquerí Indians, who could not be expected to distinguish between one Spaniard and the next. (Las Casas gives a somewhat schematic account of this on pp. 88–9.) Verapaz lasted longer, but it, too, collapsed under pressure from Spanish settlers and from the often less than peaceable ambitions of the 'honest farmers' themselves.

But for all his insistence that the Crown had seriously mismanaged its colonies and that the behaviour of the colonists had 'given reason for the name of Christ to be loathed and abominated by countless people', Las Casas never once denied, as many of his fellow-Dominicans effectively did, that the Spanish Crown was the legitimate ruler of the Americas and he persisted until his death in the belief that the indigenous peoples had, in ignorance but in good faith, voluntarily surrendered their natural sovereignty to the King of Spain. In a tract entitled *Comprobatory Treatise on the Imperial Sovereignty and Universal Jurisdiction which the Kings of Castile Have over these Indies*, printed in the same year as the *Short Account*, and probably in an attempt to deflect official criticism from it, Las Casas set out to 'silence those who say that, because I detest and severely abominate all that has happened in the Indies – as I do, and intend to do as long as I live – I thereby somehow impugn and detract from the aforesaid title'. The argument which ran through this and so many of his other quasi-legal works was simple: the kings of Spain are the legitimate rulers of the Americas; but they are so because – and *only* because – in 1493 Pope Alexander VI 'donated' to the Catholic monarchs Ferdinand and Isabella sovereignty over all the new-found lands in the Atlantic which had not already been occupied by some other Christian prince.

There were many (many of them close associates of Las Casas) who denied that the papal claim to 'plenitude of power' over the entire world, and with it the right to give away the lands of pagan princes, was a valid one. Las Casas never questioned it. It was, as he said time and again, the only possible legitimation of the Spanish presence in the Americas. But although the papal grant might confer sovereignty over the New World upon the Catholic monarchs, it did not confer property rights over the persons or lands of its inhabitants. These, he insisted, remained theirs by natural right. Nor did it entirely deprive the native rulers of their political authority. As Las Casas stated explicitly in the very last work he wrote, *On Royal Power*, the 'kings' and 'princes' of the Americas enjoyed the same status as the nobility in Naples and Milan, both of which also formed part of the Spanish Empire at this time. Furthermore, Alexander VI had charged the Catholic monarchs to 'induce the peoples who live in such islands and lands to receive the Catholic religion, save that you never inflict upon them hardships and dangers'. The Indians were not chattels or goods; they were subjects of the Castilian Crown – 'our subjects and our vassals', as Queen Isabella herself had phrased it. For the Spaniards to treat them like animals was thus against God's laws, the laws of nature, and a violation of the laws of Castile. It was also an abomination in God's eyes: a denial of the humanity which all men, whatever their beliefs or cultural preferences, shared. Las Casas was even prepared to argue, both in the *Short Account* (p. 70) and later and at greater length in *On Royal Power*, that the Indians now had sufficient cause, 'under natural, divine, and Roman law', for *them* to wage a 'just war' against the Spaniards.

Las Casas's entire life was dedicated to demonstrating the truth of these claims, first to his king, then to the royal administration – the Council of the Indies – and then to the world at large. As he stated in the preamble to his will, 'I have had no other interests but this: to liberate [the Indians] from the violent deaths which they have suffered and suffer ... through compassion at seeing so many multitudes of people who are rational, docile, humble, gentle and simple, who are so well equipped to receive our Holy Catholic Faith and every moral doctrine and who are endowed with such good customs, as God is my witness.' In pursuit of these ends Las Casas wrote a vast number of works. The bulk of these consisted of detailed and endlessly reiterated proposals for legal and institutional reform. They included, however, in addition to the *Short Account*, two further descriptive works: a massive *History of the Indies* and an equally immense work of comparative ethnology, significantly entitled *Apologetic History of the Indies*.

The *History of the Indies* contains most of the material to be found in the *Short Account*. It was, said Las Casas, 'a book of the greatest and ultimate necessity', and it had been written to demonstrate that there was no people on earth, no matter how seemingly 'barbarous' their condition, that could be denied membership of the 'Christian family'. The *History* can be read, partly as a narrative, much of it first-hand, of the discovery and conquest of the Indies, partly as a record of the Spaniards' subsequent bloody exploits, and partly as an autobiographical account of the passage of its author from ignorance to enlightenment. In 1559, however, Las Casas forbade the printing, or even the circulation of the manuscript, until forty years after his death. Then, he said, it might be printed 'if it is thought to be convenient for the good of the Indians and of Spain'. But by 1590 Spain's position was too perilous for it to be conceivable that any further condemnation of its agents could be thought to be 'for its good' and the text was not published until 1875.

II

Bartolomé de Las Casas – or Casaus, as he sometimes styled himself – was born in Seville in 1484, the son of a merchant from Tarifa and 'a woman from Sosa' who died when he was still a child. Although he has left a detailed account of his adult life in the *History of the Indies,* he is silent about his childhood and says nothing about his education. This is perhaps no accident. Las Casas had a clear idea of narrative purpose. Despite the pretence that it was nothing more than a factual record of events, the *History*, no less than the *Short Account*, was intended to persuade his king to act. Unlike the *Short Account*, however, it was also intended as a monument to Las Casas's untiring efforts on behalf of the Indians. The story of his life before his arrival in the Indies is thus irrelevant. For Las Casas, as for so many other Europeans, the crossing to America came to seem something of a rebirth. Although he was to cross and re-cross the Atlantic several times in the pursuit of his objective, it was the first voyage which ultimately determined what that objective was to be. It was, as he was to say later, God's decision that he should go to America. God had given to him 'the zeal and the desire to bring about a remedy to those wretched beings, and with these

He had given him also great perseverance'. What had happened to him in the Old World before was thus of no significance. All he tells us is that he reached Santo Domingo in what is now Haiti on 15 April 1502, in the largest fleet ever to leave Spain for the New World, and that as he landed he was told, 'You have arrived at a good moment . . . there is to be a war against the Indians and we will be able to take many slaves'. 'This news,' he later recalled in bitterness, 'produced a great joy in the ship.' It was his first encounter, although it would be a long time before he came to recognize it as such, with the realities of the colonial experience.

A year later Las Casas was moderately well-off and the master of a number of Indians. He was also in minor orders and by 1510 he had become a priest. Throughout the account he gives of this part of his life in the *History* he refers to himself, half ironically, as 'the cleric Las Casas'. Why he chose the priesthood we do not know and he does not say. The secular clergy (as distinct from members of the monastic orders) were regarded at this time, often rightly, as ignorant, poor and frequently polygamous. The narrative offered by the *History* aims to convey a sense of humility, doubtless quite genuine, and his position as a humble cleric may have seemed morally more compelling than that of the relative comfort of the monk. But there was another reason: as a member of the lay clergy he could come and go as he pleased. When in 1522 Domingo de Betanzos attempted to persuade him to enter the Dominican Order and to participate in the evangelization of the Americas he at first declined, saying that as his whole life until then had been dedicated to reform, he had to wait in the vicinity of the court until he had received his instructions from the King. Betanzos, who knew that those who wait on kings can wait for ever, asked him, 'And if you should die before then, who will receive the orders from the King?' These words, he claims, 'transfixed his heart' and he gave his previous life up for dead. It was, in its way, a conversion; one that would transform him from a self-marginalized agitator for reform into something greater and, for the Spanish colonist, far more menacing: the 'Defender of the Indians'. In his own estimation of his achievement, never slight, it was he who was subsequently responsible for 'moving all the religious of Castile, in particular those of the Orders of Saint Francis and Saint Dominic, to pass over here, where all that is required is good workmen to gather in Christ's corn'.

Unlike his reception in the Dominican Order, Las Casas's ordination seems to have had no immediate impact on his life. Like other unordained colonists, he lived from the labour of the Indians who had been 'given' him by the governor of Hispaniola, Nicolás de Ovando. In an attempt to prevent the settlers from creating feudal fiefs in America, the Catholic monarchs, Ferdinand and Isabella, had decreed that, while all land would remain the possession of the Crown, the Indians would be compelled to work it on behalf of the colonists. In exchange for their labour they would be offered the protection of the Castilian Crown, instruction in the Christian faith and a small wage. In practice, however, although they did not actually live in the colonists' households, such Indians were virtual slaves. This institution was known as the *encomienda*, because the Indians had been 'encommended' into the care of their Spanish overlord who was thus known as their *encomendero*. Las Casas came to abominate the system – a 'mortal pestilence,' he called it, 'which daily consumes these people' – and was to dedicate most of his life to its abolition. Nevertheless, at this stage, although of a 'compassionate nature' and, as he is at pains to point out, more gentle in the treatment of his Indians than most of the colonists, he had not given much thought to the matter. On the Sunday before Christmas 1511, however, the Spanish population of Hispaniola received a rude shock, which marked the beginning of Las Casas's brief and dramatic conversion from colonizing priest into Indian apostle.

The story is now a famous one. That morning a recent arrival on the island, the Dominican Antonio Montesinos, delivered a sermon in the church of Santo Domingo. Taking his text from St John, he drew an analogy between the natural desert in which the Evangelist had chosen to spend his life and the human desert which the Spaniards had made of the once fruitful, 'paradisiacal' island of Hispaniola. He then turned upon the colonists. 'With what right,' he demanded of them, 'and with what justice do you keep these poor Indians in such cruel and horrible servitude? By what authority have you made such detestable wars against these people who lived peacefully and gently on their own lands? Are these not men? Do they not have rational souls? Are you not obliged to love them as yourselves?' The last three questions were to become the referents of every subsequent struggle to defend the rights of the indigenous peoples of the Americas. For Las Casas, in particular, the third – 'Are you not obliged to love them as yourselves?' – was to guide his actions for the rest of his life.

The immediate response of 'the cleric Las Casas' to Montesinos's sermon was, nevertheless, unremarkable. He did not share the indignation of the rest of the colony, which demanded Montesinos's recantation and immediate repatriation to Spain. But neither does he seem to have grasped immediately that the full implication of what Montesinos had said was that 'one could not in conscience possess Indians' and still claim to be a Christian. Later that same year he accompanied Diego Velázquez to Cuba, where he witnessed, seemingly for the first time, the massacres which he was to describe so vividly in the *Short Account*. Although Las Casas was careful to point out how much better his behaviour was towards the Indians than that of any of his fellow-conquerors and how they came to him because of 'the great pain and pity' with which their plight filled him, and although – or so he tells us (p. 29) – he remonstrated furiously against the atrocities committed by Pánfilo de Narváez in Caonao, he served Velázquez well enough to be granted a large *encomienda* in Canarreo, near the port of Xaguá.

Las Casas's conversion did not come until three years later

and, significantly, it was the consequence not of an encounter with an individual, nor of the divine illumination which had struck Paul to the ground on the way to Damascus (he was too humble to claim that, although there are unmistakable analogies between his conversion and Paul's), nor even of direct experience of the misery of the Indians, although, as he says, he had seen much of that. It was the consequence of an encounter with a text. Paul had been struck directly by the voice of God. Las Casas, who could make no such claim, was struck by the written word, Ecclesiasticus 34: 21–2, which he 'began to consider' in preparation for his Easter sermon. 'The bread of the needy is their life,' he read, 'he that defraudeth him thereof is a man of blood. He that taketh away his neighbour's living slayeth him, and he that defraudeth the labourer of his hire is a bloodshedder.' It was this that led him 'to consider the misery and slavery that those peoples suffered', and which drew his mind back to Montesinos's sermon. He spent, he says, many days agonizing over the issue until he had 'determined within himself of the same truth, that everything which had been done to the Indians in the Indies was unjust and tyrannical'. This conclusion, too, possessed textual authority and could be checked against 'every book' he had read 'in either Latin or the vernacular, which in forty-four years were infinite'. None of these, he now noticed, could provide any legitimation for 'the condemnation and the injustice and the harm that they, the Indians, have been done'. He then announced to the astonished Velázquez that he intended to renounce 'his' Indians, although, as he admits, this could hardly have been in their interest since he was a far better master than any they were likely to acquire subsequently. Las Casas spent a further year in Cuba and in September 1515, together with Antonio Montesinos himself, he returned to Spain, determined to inform the King of the evils which his agents were perpetrating in his Indies.

Shortly before Christmas 1515, Las Casas was granted an audience with the ageing Ferdinand the Catholic and, by his own account, lectured him at great length of what 'he had seen', in the language of loss, destruction and greed which was to dominate all his later accounts. 'He informed the King of the perdition of these lands and violent death of their native inhabitants and the manner in which the Spaniards in their greed slew them, and how all died without having been baptized or having received the Sacraments and if, in brief, His Highness did not remedy the situation everything would become as a desert.'

Ferdinand, for whom the Americas were still a remote and insignificant part of his political burden, referred the matter to the president of the Council of the Indies, Juan Rodríguez de Fonseca, bishop of Burgos, a man for whom Las Casas was to conceive an abiding hatred. Fonseca, on being told of the slaughter in Cuba of seven thousand children in three months, replied, 'and how does that concern me?' For Las Casas this was a significant moment. For the rest of his very long life (he died in 1576 at the age of 92), although he collaborated with the Council wherever possible and, after 1543, was permitted to attend Council meetings, he directed all his moral energy at the members of the missionary Orders, at the Crown and, in the *Short Account*, at the international community – the Christian 'congregation of the faithful' – in the hope that the moral indignation of decent men, if sufficiently aroused, could be made to counter political and economic interests of ever-increasing complexity.

It was a naive project and, despite a vast body of legislation aimed at curbing the excesses of the settlers and for which Las Casas was at least partially responsible, it did little in the long run to alleviate the burden of the Indians. If Cortés in Mexico and Pizarro in Peru were ultimately less destructive than Velázquez had been in Cuba, this was because these self-styled conquistadores had come not merely for gold but for land. They had come to create a feudal society over which they could rule, and a feudal society required a labouring class. But if Las

Casas's efforts were largely ineffectual in practice, few of those who listened to him were so deaf as the bishop of Burgos had been. He had, indeed, throughout his life a large and powerful audience. In 1543 he was created bishop of Chiapas in southern Mexico after having, characteristically, refused the see of Cuzco, 'the richest in all the Indies'. He had, too, friends who were as powerful as his detractors. On one occasion no less a person than the archbishop of Toledo, the primate of Spain, Bartolomé de Carranza, had to be forcibly separated from the jurist Pedro de Castro 'because of the book which the bishop of Chiapas had written about the affairs of the Indies'.

Las Casas was always able to play upon a deep moral unease within royal and ecclesiastical circles. The Spanish Crown had a long history of anxiety over the legitimacy of its military ventures and ever since the twelfth century Castilian monarchs had sought the advice of jurists and theologians as to how to conduct, or to seem to conduct, their affairs. They may not have always taken this advice too literally for, as the greatest of the Spanish theologians of the sixteenth century Francisco de Vitoria once observed, kings are necessarily pragmatic beings forced 'to think from hand to mouth'. But the Spanish monarchs, the self-styled champions of Christendom, lived in constant fear of finding themselves out of favour with their God. It is not surprising, then, that even before Montesinos had delivered his famous sermon there had been questions asked about the legitimacy of Spanish activities in the Indies.

In 1513, in an attempt to silence any further protest, the jurist Juan López de Palacios Rubios, one of King Ferdinand's ideologues, drew up a document known as the 'Requirement' (or *Requerimiento*). This began with a history of the world since Adam. It then moved swiftly on to the grant made by the Pope to the Castilian Crown and the obligation of every Indian to pay homage to the agents of the Crown and to obey their orders. It finished with a gruesome account of what would befall any Indian who refused to obey. Every conquistador was to carry a copy of this document with him and to read it, in the presence of a notary, before making an attack. The facts that the document was in Spanish, a language no Indian could then understand, that it made no attempt to explain the complex legal and theological terms in which it was expressed, and that it was frequently read at night to sleeping villages or out of earshot of the Indians (see pp. 33 and 56) were disregarded. What mattered was the act. Once the Europeans had discharged their duty to inform, the way was clear for pillage and enslavement. When asked what he thought of this, surely one of the crassest instances of legalism in European history, Las Casas replied that he did not know whether to laugh or to cry. But the *Requerimiento* was taken seriously enough. Pedrarias Dávila's expedition to Tierra Firme in 1513 (see p. 31) was held up for months while the document was drafted.

That same year, in an attempt to regulate the relations between the colonizer and the colonized, the Crown drafted its first major legislation, the Laws of Burgos. These, in addition to forbidding Spaniards to address Indians as 'dogs', attempted to limit the number of hours local people might be required to work, ensure that they were adequately fed and provide them with proper instruction in the Christian faith. Although Las Casas welcomed these laws as evidence of the Crown's 'kindly intentions' towards its new vassals, they clearly did not go far enough. The Indians still remained bound to their masters, deprived of what not only Las Casas but most of the missionaries considered to be their natural rights to property. Worse still, the laws made provision for the creation of new Indian settlements close to the Spanish towns. This forceful disruption of the older tribal lifestyles was thought necessary because the Indians, whose 'sole aim and pleasure in life is to have the freedom to do with themselves exactly as they please', not surprisingly showed little pleasure in the company of Spaniards and would otherwise 'forsake conversation and communication with Christians and flee into the jungle'. Although it is never mentioned by Las Casas, his gaze forever fixed upon atrocities that could be rendered arithmetically, the dissolution of tribal unity and of the group's sense of its own social cohesion which these moves inevitably created, together with the crude attempts to impose such things as Christian marriage, European dress, and Spanish eating-habits, contributed significantly to the dramatic decline in the population of the Indies. The cultural and social demands of the *encomienda* may indeed have been responsible for many of those features of Indian life which the Europeans found most reprehensible, suicide, infanticide and induced abortion, and for what another of Las Casas's enemies, the chronicler Gonzalo Fernández de Oviedo, referred to as the Indians' 'lack of charity' – their apparent willingness to abandon the sick and the old and to mock the sufferings of the dying. Extremes of cultural dislocation can lead to terrifying reversals in human relations. Similar behaviour was observed on the Franciscan mission stations in California in the eighteenth century – places more reminiscent of forced-labour camps than of centres of Christian instruction – and were noted again in the 1960s among the Ik, an East-African people displaced from their tribal homelands and their traditional means of subsistence by the creation of a game reserve.

The Laws of Burgos led to the disruption of Indian life, but they achieved little else. Unpopular legislation was always impossible to enforce in the Indies. The coercive powers of the Castilian Crown were over-extended and the problems in Europe – the need to defend Spain and southern Italy from infiltration by Protestants and attack from the Turks – always took first place. The Americas also attracted the kind of settlers who wished to set themselves up in imitation of a society to which they had had no access in Europe. For them the Indians were a crucial part of their social reconstruction of themselves. Men, they knew, became masters only when they had other men to command. If the Crown threatened to deprive them of the substance of their dream, they could, as Cortés's lieutenant Cristóbal de Olid had done in Honduras (see p. 54) and Lope de Aguirre was to attempt to do in the Amazon, create independent kingdoms in the jungle for themselves – those hallucinatory empires which still haunt much modern Latin-American fiction. Faced with the serious possibility of a full-scale rebellion of this kind, the Crown was always ready to back down.

The next, and the final, attempt to regulate the behaviour of the colonists, and to confer some measure of political rights upon the Indians, met with a similar fate. The New Laws of 1542, unlike the Laws of Burgos, owe something to Las Casas. These, he said of them in the *Short Account*, 'provide, in the most efficacious manner the drafters have been able to devise, for the eradication of the evils and godless crimes perpetrated against Our Lord and our fellow-human beings' (p. 128). Had they been in any lasting sense effective, they would have constituted the legislative expression of his endless programmes for reform, for they went far further than the Laws of Burgos had done. They revised and extended the judicial system in the Americas, they limited the amount any Indian could be asked to carry, and they freed all but a small number of Indian slaves. Crucially, they stipulated that as each current holder of an *encomienda* died, his grant would revert to the Crown. Within a generation the Indians would have become full subjects of the Castilian Crown, the bearers of the same rights as the Spaniards themselves, and the loathed *encomienda* would be at an end. However, as Las Casas himself records, the New Laws were met at first by disbelief – 'Is this,' one colonist conventionally demanded, 'how the King rewards his loyal subjects?' – then by the threat and in Peru by the reality of revolt and finally, in 1545, by their partial repeal.

But if Las Casas's labours had no lasting impact upon colonial legislation, his influence at a less immediate level was immense. He was and remains to this day the moral conscience of the 'enterprise of the Indies'. Not only did he agitate for the rights and better treatment of the Indians but he also defended their claim, which in the Spain of the mid-sixteenth century was constantly under surveillance, to be regarded as human beings. Ever since 1513, Las Casas had fought against the suggestion that the Indians might be some species of sub-human, the 'natural slaves' which Aristotle had suggested might exist somewhere in the world for the benefit of civilized men. His longest and most original work, the *Apologetic History of the Indies*, a vast comparative ethnology of the Americas, is precisely an extended attempt to demonstrate, beyond all shadow of empirical doubt, that the Indians were fully rational beings with a culture which, though certainly 'primitive' in its technology and in a large number of its cultural practices, was equal to anything which the Old World had produced. The *Apologetic History* was also the product of the most famous – if also still the most ill-understood – moment of conflict between Las Casas and his opponents, which took place just one year before the *Short Account* was printed.

In 1548, two of Spain's most prominent theologians from the University of Salamanca, Melchor Cano and Bartolomé de Carranza, together with the jurist Diego de Covarrubias, were asked by the Crown, which frequently employed theologians and jurists for this task, to examine a work in dialogue form entitled *The Second Democrates; Or, The Just Causes of the War against the Indians*. Its author, Juan Ginés de Sepúlveda, was one of Charles V's chaplains and his official chronicler. Its cryptic title referred, significantly, to an earlier work, *The First Democrates*, which had attempted to justify the sack of Rome in 1527 by Charles V's mutinous armies. It was one of the most virulent onslaughts on the Indians ever written. The Indians were, said its author, '*homunculi* in whom hardly a vestige of humanity remains'. They were 'like pigs with their eyes always fixed on the ground'. Their brutish behaviour, absence of any recognizable culture, their cowardice (had not Montezuma, reputed to be 'the bravest among them', capitulated to Cortés without protest?), their supposed cannibalism and their paganism, all clearly indicated that God had intended them to be slaves to those whose 'magna-

nimity, temperance, humanity and religion' — by whom
Sepúlveda meant the Spaniards — made them their natural masters. The theologians claimed that the book was doctrinally
unsound, the work of a man who, while he was probably a good
Latin stylist, was a poor logician and a worse theologian, and
they recommended that it should be denied the royal licence
without which no book could legally be printed in Spain.

Their reasons for condemning Sepúlveda's work were several.
Its tone clearly offended them, as did most of the arguments it
employed, and they believed that the circulation of such an
obviously inflammatory text could only have exacerbated the
running battle between the colonists and the religious orders.
But both Carranza and Cano were, like Las Casas, Dominicans,
and both were acquaintances of Las Casas. Sepúlveda, therefore
and not unreasonably, assumed that it was Las Casas who had
been ultimately responsible for his humiliation. His book, he
told Antoine Perrenot de Granvelle, who was then Charles V's
first minister in Augsburg, 'had been approved by all those
learned men who read it without passion before the bishop of
Chiapas took it upon himself to weave the web he wove in
Salamanca'. Sepúlveda pressed his case with the Council of the
Indies which, in August 1550, organized a 'debate' between the
two men under the aegis of, among others, Cano, Carranza, and
another eminent theologian, Domingo de Soto. It was a curious
event. Las Casas clearly had not read Sepúlveda's original text
but only a later summary, and, oddly for a 'debate', on no
occasion did the two participants actually meet. Each contestant
read his objections to the panel and of these Soto compiled,
somewhat against his will, a faithful record. Las Casas began by
reading, for days on end, a long rambling text, the *Apologetic
Argument against Ginés de Sepúlveda* in which he set out to refute
not only the substance of *The Second Democrates* but, as Soto drily
observed, 'everything that the doctor Sepúlveda had ever written'. In April of the following year Sepúlveda countered with
twelve replies to this, and Las Casas then replied with twelve

objections to the replies. That was all. There was no outcome to the affair – unless the theologians' refusal to change their minds about the subversive nature of Sepúlveda's original text can be considered an outcome. But then no outcome was expected. The purpose of the exercise was almost entirely ceremonial. Like the meetings (*juntas*) of theologians and jurists which the Crown frequently convened to discuss delicate political matters and which in so many ways it resembled, the 'debate' had allowed full and exact expression to be given to the views of both sides. It was up to the Council of the Indies to act.

Inconclusive though it was in all other respects, the Valladolid debate was an important event in Las Casas's life. It was his last major encounter with his intellectual opponents, and it may also explain why he decided to publish the *Short Account* the following year. For one of the major themes which dominate his objection to Sepúlveda's text is its persistent and malign distortion of the nature of Indian society. This, Las Casas argued, was due to personal ignorance of the place and to Sepúlveda's reliance on that 'cruel enemy of the Indians', Fernández de Oviedo who, although he had lived in America, had only ever seen what he, Indian slaver and *encomendero* as he was, wished to see. For, like all of Las Casas's writings, but more strikingly, more urgently than any other, the *Short Account* was an attempt to press upon the reader the immediacy of the American experience, the importance of 'being there', and of being there with innocent intentions.

III

The *Short Account* is, as Las Casas claims (p. 4), an epitome, suitably re-worded for a popular audience, of the records of Spanish brutality given in the *History*, together with some gory details of its own. The purposes of the two works were, as he made clear in the prologue to the *History*, identical. Both were true and unembellished records of what had been seen by him and by those he knew. Unlike the *History*, however, the *Short Account* is, by implication at least, a *relación* – the name given to the official report, witnessed and authenticated by a notary, which every royal officer in the Indies was expected to provide of his activities. Hernán Cortés's massively over-extended letters to Charles V were described by their author as 'letters of account' (*cartas de relación*), thus suggesting that, despite their narrative structure and epistolary form, their *content* possessed all the accuracy of a legal document. Las Casas's title was intended to convey the same impression. The aims of Cortés and Las Casas could not have been more different, but their rhetorical strategies were, unsurprisingly perhaps since both men inhabited the same political and literary culture, very similar. Like Cortés's *Letters*, the *Short Account*, in its final printed form, was meant in the first instance for a royal reader, in this case the future Philip II, before whom it would have been unthinkable to lie. Like Cortés's *Letters* it was intended not merely to inform but to persuade. It was in the most immediate, most transparent sense of the word, an exercise in propaganda. Many of the stories which Las Casas told may, indeed, have literally been true. Some of them, the numbing round of killings, beatings, rapes and enslavements, certainly were. But others, such as the story of the Spaniard who stopped the mouths of the prisoners he was torturing with wooden bungs so as not to disturb his commander's siesta (p. 16), have classical antecedents and constitute part of a recognizable rhetorical strategy for arousing wonder in the reader. The same is true of Las Casas's figures. These begin as precise accounts – the population of the Mexican town of Cholula, for instance, is given as 'some thirty thousand inhabitants' (p. 45), – balanced estimates – 'at a conservative estimate . . . more than twelve million souls, women and children among them' (p. 12) – and then slide, as the work reaches its conclusion, into the indeterminacy of 'teeming millions' (p. 127). A lot of energy, most of it wasted, has been spent on verifying (or falsifying) the number of the dead given in the *Short Account*. But, quite apart from the fact that *all* such figures in the sixteenth century were, of necessity, very approximate, Las Casas's figures, always rounded up to the nearest thousand, were not offered as a factual record. As with the Roman historian Flavius Josephus's account of the destruction of Jerusalem by Titus, which Las Casas cites at length in the prologue to the *History* (and as, indeed, with Cortés's own account of the size of the native armies he had to face), the inflation of numbers was meant only to impress upon the reader the literal magnitude of the event.

Like Cortés's *Letters*, Las Casas's *Short Account* also constituted a petition. But whereas Cortés's was a petition for honours, Las Casas's was a petition for justice. His motive for writing the work was, as it was with the *History*, 'the very great and final need to make known to all Spain the true account and truthful understanding of what I have seen take place in this Indian Ocean'. He was, he claimed, the only reliable witness to what had occurred in the Americas 'wherever Christians have set foot', for only he had been willing to break the 'conspiracy of silence about what has really been happening'. 'It has become the custom,' he complained, 'to falsify the reports sent back to Spain about the damaging nature of Spanish actions in the New World.' Those few who, like himself, were prepared to risk official disapproval and, more dangerous still, the fury of the settlers, found that their 'reliable eye-witness accounts' were 'totally discounted' by indifferent royal auditors who returned statements which were at best 'hazy and unspecific' and were always more concerned with any financial loss to the Crown than they were with the ceaseless haemorrhage of human life. Only his own *Short Account* was true, not only because it did not fudge the facts but because it alone dealt with the one feature of the Spanish settlement of America which mattered: 'the massacres of innocent people'. These were, he claimed, of such magnitude that not only did they 'silence all talk of other wonders of the world', they also threatened to destroy the existing world order, 'to bring a collapse of civilization and to presage the end of the world'. Little wonder, then, that when Las Casas told his story to those he met in Spain, they 'listened open-mouthed to his every word' (p. 3).

Las Casas's task, as he saw it, was to bear witness. He was, he asserted again and again, a recorder, an historian in the proper, ancient sense of that term. In the prologue to the *History* – a long, somewhat disjointed essay on the identity and purpose of the historian's task – he stated that the majority of the historians of antiquity had written either out of the desire to demonstrate their eloquence, or out of a need to glorify their rulers. (So, too, Las Casas implied, had all the other historians of the Indies, in particular Fernández de Oviedo.) Those who escaped this fate fell into two categories. There were some, like the Greek Diodorus Siculus who, because they had been present at all that they described, had been able, as Diodorus put it, to provide 'the reader, through such a presentation of events, with the most excellent kind of experience'. And then there were those, like Josephus, the historian of another race (the Jews) who had been destroyed by a rapacious imperial power, who had written 'to bear witness to great and noteworthy deeds for the benefit of many': great and noteworthy deeds which the official record would prefer to have silently forgotten or presented as something other than what they were. In Las Casas's writings the two objectives were merged. He wrote to reveal the truth of what had been hidden and, like Diodorus ('more like a holy theologian than a damned pagan philosopher'), he, too, had 'been there'; he, too, could transmute the narrative of what he had seen into a mode of experience.

Las Casas's claim for these two aspects of his works can be repeatedly found in nearly all of them. In part this was, as we have seen, a claim to be the only one willing to speak out about matters others would prefer to leave hidden. In part, however, it marked the beginning of a divide, which was to characterize most subsequent writings about the Americas, between those who had and those who had not been there. In the mid-sixteenth century, this distinction was far less obviously significant than it would be today. In the intellectual world to which Las Casas belonged it was believed that the nature of the universe and of man could be known only through a body of authoritative texts – the Bible, the writings of the Church Fathers and a select number of ancient authors – and through commentaries on those texts. The gathering of empirical data was only of secondary importance and, by and large, had to be fitted into a framework already established by the texts. When America was discovered every attempt was made to find a place for it in classical and biblical schemes of classification. Unknown plants, such as tobacco, were given a place in a natural history which derived from the work of Dioscorides, a first-century Greek physician. The religion of the Indians was treated as a corrupt or perverted form of Christianity or, in some cases, of Judaism. Even the continent itself was located, as best it could, within the Ptolemaic world picture which, of course, allowed for the existence of only three continents and one ocean.

For those who had been to America, however, the very newness of the New World was not something which could be so casually overlooked. The missionaries, in particular, were often acutely aware of the distance, geographical and conceptual, they had had to travel. In a dialogue written in 1551 by the Franciscan Pedro de Quiroga for the instruction of his fellow-missionaries, the principal speaker, Barchilón, warns his friend Justino who has just arrived from Spain: 'Have no dealings with the things of this land until you understand them, because they are strange affairs and a strange language which only experience will reveal to you.' Quiroga, like Las Casas, knew that in America nothing was ever quite what it seemed, particularly if you went expecting it to be not very different from Europe. You had, as Barchilón implied, to learn how to speak again as you had as a child, through direct and immediate contact with the things of the world. Until and unless you had mastered this new speech America would remain a massive, frequently threatening presence which could all too easily overwhelm the imagination.

A similar sense of the weight of the new is proclaimed in the very first sentence of the *Short Account*. The discovery and subsequent Spanish occupation, Las Casas cautions his readers, will seem 'quite incredible to anyone who has not experienced it at first hand'. This is a familiar plea to the reader's trust. But a sense of the distances which separated the impact of the unmediated experience from what could only be known through language was a feature of all the early chronicles of the Indies. Oviedo declared that he would need a Leonardo da Vinci or a Mantegna or a Berruguete – 'famous painters,' he added, flaunting his European culture, 'whom I met in Italy' – to render accurately the flora of Hispaniola. Alonso de Zuazo, a judge on the island of Cuba, abandoned his attempt to describe the goods on sale in the market in Mexico City because, he explained, 'you will not gain thereby any understanding of the quality of the fruit, for such cannot be understood without the senses of sight, smell, and taste'. As Michel de Certeau has observed of such claims, 'only the appeal to the senses . . . and a link to the body . . . seem capable of bringing closer and guaranteeing, in a single but indisputable fashion, the real that is lost in language'. It was precisely the 'real that is lost in language' which Las Casas, in both the *Short Account* and the *History*, attempted so painfully to transcribe.

History of the kind Las Casas wrote was the crucial exception to the notion of a text-bound science. Las Casas specifically repudiated textual knowledge. 'I am,' he told Charles V's minister, the Seigneur de Chièvres, 'the oldest of those who went over to the Indies and, in the many years that I have been there and in which I have seen with my eyes, I have not read histories which could be lies but instead I have experienced.' The narratives which the *History* provides are 'true' precisely because they are the record of things which the historian himself has seen. The Greek word *historein*, said Las Casas, quoting the great seventh-century encyclopaedist, St Isidore of Seville, 'means "see" or "know"', and, among the ancients, only those who had witnessed, or who had seen with their own eyes what they recounted, wrote history. We know those things which we have seen with our own eyes better than those which we know by hearsay. The true historian is a witness. 'Only I,' Las Casas told the Council of the Indies, who have been 'an eye-witness for all the years since they [the Americas] were discovered', who have 'wandered through these Indies since very nearly the year 1500', could be trusted to 'know what I write'. The eye, which offers direct access to the world of experience, takes priority over the ear and, because what it sees is both transparent and innocent, the witness it bears is exempt from interpretation. But, of course, the witness's experience had to be transmuted *into* text. The only science which provided any guidelines as to how to do *that* was the law and it is, therefore, unsurprising that much of the rhetoric, and some of the compositional strategies of Las Casas's writings, are so clearly indebted to forensic practice. As with the record of any judicial procedure, the process of transmuting direct testimony into language must, inevitably, result in a text which is uneven and, in Las Casas's word, 'uncured'. The very roughness of the historian's prose thus becomes evidence of the directness of his speech. The appeal to precisely those features of the text which, in any other circumstances, would have reduced its value in the reader's eyes becomes what in the elaborate language of sixteenth-century rhetoric was known as 'capturing the good will of the reader' (*captatio benevolentiae*). The 'poverty of vocabulary and humility of the style' of the *History* is, said Las Casas, proof of both accuracy and sincerity. Here, his Italian translator claimed of the *Short Account*, is a work 'which looks only at the simple naked truth – at the facts – without caring for method or for eloquence of any kind'.

Like most instances of *captatio benevolentiae*, however, these assertions are very largely false. Las Casas, it is true, was not an elegant prose stylist. And many of his writings were, indeed, 'uncured'. But both the *Short Account* and the *History*, intended as they were for large general audiences, were carefully composed to make the 'simple naked truth' not merely evident but also compelling. Nor is it, of course, the case that Las Casas was present at all the events he describes. He witnessed the conquest of Cuba and was present on the mainland of Venezuela and parts of Mexico. But he never set foot in the areas of the largest, most devastating conquests, Central Mexico and Peru. When dealing with these areas then, he substitutes another's eyes for his own. 'I was told', 'I heard it from one who was there', 'he told me so', and similar phrases are used to punctuate the narrative. Sometimes, too, he incorporates entire documents into the texts. The Franciscan Marcos de Niza's account of the killing of the Inca Atahualpa, for instance (which Las Casas reproduces on pp. 110–14), is in effect a deposition, a sworn testimony written precisely by one who had 'first-hand experience of these people' and was thus able to bear 'true witness'. So, too, is the letter of 1541 from the bishop of Santa Marta to the King (pp. 81–4).

But Las Casas, and those of his associates like Marcos de Niza, was not only *there*. He was there with a purpose, to bear witness to that to which 'no chronicle could ever do justice, nor any reader respond to save with horror and disbelief', and to bring it back home to Spain (p. 25). For forty-two years, he says at the end of the *Short Account*, 'these matters have been constantly before my eyes and on my mind' (p. 125). Before he had gone to America and returned, the Spaniards had known nothing of the lands their fellow-nationals were in the process of destroying. 'I can swear before God,' he wrote in 1535, 'that, until I went to this royal court, even in the time when the Catholic king Don Ferdinand was still alive, no one knew what thing the Indies were, nor of their greatness, their opulence, their prosperity' – nor, he added, 'of the destruction which had been wrought in them'.

The *Short Account* was intended to alert the King's moral imagination in the hope that the Crown might act to save the Americas before it was too late. But it had another overt purpose. 'My deep love of Castile,' he wrote at the very end of the work, 'has also been a spur, for I do not wish to see my country destroyed as a divine punishment for sins against the honour of God and the true Faith' (p. 127). So far, God had confined himself to sinking Spanish treasure ships and fomenting civil war in judgement on 'the great iniquities committed by the Spanish' (pp. 19–20). But Las Casas remained certain until his death that God had more terrible punishments in store for Spain, if the Spaniards continued with the wanton destruction of His people. 'I believe,' he stated in his will, 'that because of these impious and ignominious deeds, so unjust, tyrannical and barbarously done in the Indies and against the Indians, God must certainly envelop Spain with his fury and his anger'. The use of the term 'destruction' in the title of the *Short Account* was an implicit reference to an earlier 'destruction' of Spain, the Arab invasion of 711. And, in case Las Casas's readers were in any doubt about the association between the Muslim destruction of Spain and the Christian destruction of America, Las Casas spelled it out in a list of solutions to the Indian 'problem' known as *Among the Remedies*, printed at the same time and in some versions in the same volume as the *Short Account*. 'Spain,' he wrote, 'was destroyed once by Moors ... and it is rather to be believed that this was because of the sins of all the people and of the harm and evil they had done to their neighbours. And now we have heard many say, "Pray to God that He does not destroy Spain for the many evils which we have heard are committed in the Indies".' And, he went on, if such persons, unlearned and inexperienced, can say that, 'it must be no small warning nor small threat from God'. Las Casas's prophetic claims played upon fears which were already widespread in Spain, as the Turkish presence in the Mediterranean increased year by year. For many, and in particular for one of such an apocalyptic cast of mind as Las Casas, God's displeasure could be the only cause of the repeated successes of the Ottoman fleet and of such instances of internal unrest as the revolts of the towns (*comuneros*) of Castile against Charles V in 1520–21. Even

Spain's current financial crisis, he believed, could be seen as a portent of impending retribution.

Las Casas's explicit association between Arab conqueror and Spanish conquistadores also reversed a common stereotype. As he himself records, the conquistadores had frequently compared their activities to those of the Christian heroes of the Reconquest of Spain from the Arabs. New arrivals in the Americas often had masses said on landing for the soul of that legendary hero of the Reconquest, El Cid, thus symbolically stating their own intentions to re-enact in another place what had come to be thought of as the defining event of the Spanish past. In Las Casas's eyes these men, in the accounts they gave of their deeds, drew not only upon false analogies, they also distorted language itself. In their own estimation, they were conquistadores, conquerors. 'But this term "conquest",' wrote Las Casas in a memorandum of 1542 (compare pp. 6 and 43), 'is tyrannical, Mohammedan, abusive, improper, and infernal.' A 'conquest', he went on, can be conducted only against 'Moors from Africa, Turks and heretics who seize our lands, persecute Christians and work for the destruction of our faith'. You can only speak to the woefully under-informed of 'conquering' peoples so gentle that they would flee rather than fight, whose wars were 'no more deadly than our jousting, or than many European children's games' (p. 15) and whose arms – even those of the Inca – were 'a joke' (p. 109). 'Conquest' belonged with those other terms with which the conquistadores decorated the accounts they gave of their own deeds – with 'victories' (p. 70) which designated only massacres, 'uprisings' (p. 119) which described the Indians' terrified attempts to escape their persecutors, and 'rebellions' which denoted legitimate resistance against 'the forces of plague and carnage' (p. 121).

For Las Casas, these 'men of blood', far from being Christian knights, or the heroes of the ballads and chivalric romances which seem to have been their favourite reading, were themselves 'Moorish barbarians'. All men, as he had told Sepúlveda in 1551, no matter what their cultural origins, became barbarians when driven to perform 'cruel, inhuman, wild, and merciless acts'. In America the world had been reversed. In America, it was the Europeans, 'anaesthetized to human suffering by their own greed and ambition' (p. 3), who were the savages, and the Indians, whose culture was poor, whose technology was non-existent and who had very few, if any, of the arts and sciences which for all Europeans marked the inevitable stages towards true civility, who were 'civilized'.

It is the language of the Gospels, with its emphasis on rejection and simplicity, which allowed Las Casas to transpose the traditional relationship between 'us' and the 'other' in this way. The Indians are characterized in images which suggest both Apostolic purity and natural innocence, just as the land they inhabit is always rich in natural wealth, 'innocent' of human interference. They share with the desert Fathers poverty and an ignorance of both greed and worldly power, and they order their lives 'as honourably as might the inmates of a well-run monastery' (p. 23). Even as slaves they move, as befits Christ's creatures, in flocks. The Spaniards, by contrast, are described in the language used by the medieval chroniclers of the Arab conquerors of Christian Visigothic Spain. They, the 'Moors', are like 'ravening wolves' among 'gentle lambs', and like 'tigers and savage lions who have not eaten meat for days' (pp. 12, 58 and 96). This is at least one reason why Las Casas so rarely gives names to any of the 'butchers' whose actions he chronicles with such care, for they are not men so much as the attributes of savagery, their behaviour having rendered what were once humans, like 'us', into something wholly other. As Las Casas's own conversion had revealed to him, no man could participate in the carnage which was the conquest of America and still retain his innocence or, in the end, his humanity. 'The longer men have operated in the New World,' he observed, 'and the more they have become accustomed to the carnage and butchery around them, the more brutal and wicked have been the crimes they have committed against God and their fellow-men' (p. 103). In the end, such people cease 'to be men in any meaningful sense of the term' (p. 3). And the religion which they profess, most gentle when conveyed by Las Casas and his colleagues – those 'angels' whom the Indians welcome 'with great emotion and joy' (pp. 78 and 88–9) – becomes, itself, a profanation. The Indians can hardly be blamed if they translate 'Christian' as '*yares*, which means demons . . . in their language' (p. 82), nor if they assume Him to be the God of gold. 'Here,' Las Casas makes one Cuban chieftain say, pointing to a basket filled with gold and jewellery, 'is the God of the Christians' (p. 28).

Many Europeans had stated, and would continue to do so well into the nineteenth century, that America was, indeed, a world upside-down where, as one Spanish traveller mockingly claimed, the rivers ran inland and the women urinated standing up. If that is the case, argued Las Casas, then it is only so because of what the Europeans have done to it. It is they, little more than a 'band of fortune hunters', not the Indians, who have abandoned nature. It is they who have toppled pagan idols and replaced them with the images of Mammon. It is they who have laid waste a vast and fertile land, a territory at once richer and grander – 'the whole world,' he once wrote, 'is merely a toy compared to the world of these Indies' – than anything its readers in Europe could hope to imagine. The *Short Account* was written in protest at a moment when it still seemed possible to reverse the damage Spanish colonization had done, when it still, to Las Casas at least, seemed possible that his 'earthly paradise' might be transformed into the image of the primitive Apostolic Church. But he was already too late. By the time this book was published the destruction of the Indies was virtually complete. The Indians, their culture all but eradicated or forgotten, were already faced with the need either to become a lowly, marginalized part of the European colonial system or, as they continue to do in increasing numbers, to perish altogether.

CHRONOLOGY

1484 Las Casas born in Seville.

1492 Christopher Columbus makes first landfall in the Americas.

1493 Pope Alexander VI grants sovereignty in the Americas to the Castilian Crown.

1502 Las Casas lands at Santo Domingo on the Spanish island of Hispaniola (now Haiti).

1510 Ordained priest.

1511 Accompanies Diego Velázquez in the conquest of Cuba.

1513 Drafting of the Laws of Burgos, first attempt to regulate the behaviour of the Spanish settlers.

1515 Las Casas returns to Spain and informs King Ferdinand of the atrocities being committed in the Americas.

1519 Charles I of Spain is elected Holy Roman Emperor as Charles V.

1519–22 Hernán Cortés overruns the Aztec Empire.

1522 Las Casas returns to Hispaniola.

1523 Received into the Dominican Order.

1527 Begins work on the *Historia de las Indias*.

1525–40 Travels widely in the Americas gathering evidence of, and preaching against, Spanish mistreatment of the Indians.

1531–2 Francisco Pizarro destroys the empire of the Incas.

1542 Promulgation of the New Laws aimed at further controlling the actions of the Spanish (partially repealed in 1545).

1543 Las Casas is made Bishop of Chiapas.

1545–60 The Verapaz experiment – an attempt, masterminded by Las Casas, to settle the coast of what is now Venezuela with 'honest' Spanish farmers.

1550 Debate between Las Casas and Juan Ginés de Sepúlveda over the nature of the American Indians.

1552 Las Casas publishes the *Short Account of the Destruction of the Indies*.

1576 Death of Las Casas.

FURTHER READING

Bataillon, Marcel, *Las Casas, et la défense des indiens* (Paris, 1971)

Casas, Bartolomé de Las, *Bartolomé de Las Casas: A Selection of his Writings*, trans. and ed. George Sanderlin (New York, 1971)

Friede, Juan and Benjamin Keen, *Bartolomé de Las Casas in History: Toward an Understanding of the Man and his Work* (De Klab, 1971)

Hanke, Lewis, *Bartolomé de Las Casas: An Interpretation of his Life and Writings* (The Hague, 1951)

—, *Bartolomé de Las Casas, Bookman, Scholar, Propagandist* (Philadelphia, 1952)

—, *All Mankind is One: A Study of the Disputation Between Bartolomé de Las Casas and Juan Ginés de Sepúlveda on the Religious and Intellectual Capacity of the American Indians* (De Klab, 1974)

Manh-Lot, Marianne, *Bartolomé de Las Casas et le droit des Indiens* (Paris, 1982)

Pagden, Anthony, *The Fall of Natural Man: The American Indian and the Origins of Comparative Ethnology* (Cambridge, 1986)

Parish, Helen Rand, *Las Casas as Bishop* (Washington DC, 1980)

Saint-Lu, André, *Las Casas et la défense des Indiens* (Paris, 1971)

Scvilla-Casas, Elias (ed.), *Western Expansion and Indigenous Peoples: The Heritage of Las Casas. International Congress of Anthropological and Ethnological Sciences, Chicago 1973* (The Hague–Chicago, 1977)

Todorov, Tzvetan, *The Conquest of America: The Question of the Other*, trans. Richard Howard (Oklahoma, 1991)

Traboulay, David, *Columbus and Las Casas: The Conquest and Christianization of America 1492–1566* (Maryland, 1994)

Wagner, Henry Raup (with the collaboration of Helen Rand Parish), *The Life and Writings of Bartolomé de Las Casas* (Albuquerque, 1967)

A NOTE ON EDITIONS AND ON THIS TRANSLATION

No autograph manuscript survives of the *Short Account*. I have used the text of the first printed edition which appeared at Seville, Spain's premier port and the centre of trade with the Americas. The printer, Sebastián Trugillo, issued no fewer than eight tracts of Las Casas, among them the *Short Account*, all bearing the date 1552. A ninth came that same year from the presses of the greatest of sixteenth-century Seville printers, Jacobo Cromberger.

A facsimile of the first edition was issued by the Fundación Universitaria Española in Madrid in 1977 with Introduction and Notes by Manuel Ballesteros-Gaibrois. There is a handy modern Spanish edition of the 1552 text by André Saint-Lu in the Clásicos Cátedra series (Madrid, 1984).

The *Short Account* enjoyed a great *succès de scandale*: before the century was out translations of the work had appeared in Flemish, English, French, German, and Latin. The first English version, entitled *The Spanish Colonie* . . . , was made by one 'M. M. S.' and printed in London by Thomas Dawson for William Brome in 1583. It was this version that Samuel Purchas used in Part IV of *Purchase his Pilgrime*. Facsimiles of this translation were published in the U.S. in 1966 and 1977. A second version by 'J. P.' (John Phillips) appeared in 1656 under the title *The Tears of the Indians* (London: J.C. for Nath. Brook). A facsimile of this was issued in the 1950s, and it was also edited by Oriole Editions, as part of their Chapbook series (New York, 1970), with an introduction by Colin Steele. Six of the Trugillo 1552 tracts, among them the *Short Account*, were printed in English in 1699 (London: J. Darby for Daniel Brown and Andrew Bell).

There are two more recent English translations: one by Francis A. MacNutt (New York, 1909) and, in the March of America series, the other by Herma Briffault, with an introduction by Hans Magnus Enzensberger (New York: Seabury Press, 1974), where it is entitled *The Devastation of the Indies*. Neither is in print.

With the exception of the material cited by Las Casas from Juan Fernández de Ángulo and Marcos de Niza (pp. 81–3 and 110–14), I have retained the paragraph and chapter divisions of the 1552 printing.

Although there is a long tradition, going back to Columbus's conviction that he had found a westward passage to the Far East, of referring to the Americas as the 'Indies' and the inhabitants as 'Indians' – a tradition reflected in the historical introduction to this edition – I have chosen to use the term 'Antilles' (Spanish *Antillas*) when referring to the Indies and to translate the term 'Indians' (Spanish *indios*), as it is used by Las Casas, by a variety of less anachronistic words and phrases, such as 'Amerindians', 'natives', and 'local people'.

A SHORT ACCOUNT OF THE
DESTRUCTION OF THE INDIES

SYNOPSIS

Everything that has happened since the marvellous discovery of the Americas – from the short-lived initial attempts of the Spanish to settle there, right down to the present day – has been so extraordinary that the whole story remains quite incredible to anyone who has not experienced it at first hand. It seems, indeed, to overshadow all the deeds of famous men of the past, no matter how heroic, and to silence all talk of other wonders of the world. Prominent amid the aspects of this story which have caught the imagination are the massacres of innocent peoples, the atrocities committed against them and, among other horrific excesses, the ways in which towns, provinces, and whole kingdoms have been entirely cleared of their native inhabitants. Brother Bartolomé de Las Casas, or Casaus, came to the Spanish court after he entered the Order, to give our Lord, the Emperor, an eye-witness account of these enormities, not a whisper of which had at that time reached the ears of people here. He also related these same events to several people he met during his visit and they were deeply shocked by what he had to say and listened open-mouthed to his every word; they later begged him and pressed him to set down in writing a short account of some of them, and this he did. Some years later, he observed that not a few of the people involved in this story had become so anaesthetized to human suffering by their own greed and ambition that they had ceased to be men in any meaningful sense of the term and had become, by dint of their own wicked deeds, so totally degenerate and given over to a reprobate mind[1] that they could

---

1 Romans 1: 28: 'And even as they did not like to retain God in *their* knowledge, God gave them over to a reprobate mind.' The phrase is used twice more later in the work (see below, pp. 69 and 74)

not rest content with their past achievements in the realms of treachery and wickedness (when they honed to perfection the art of cruelty in order to wipe human beings from a large part of the globe), but were now pestering the Crown to grant them official authority and licence once again to commit their dreadful deeds, or even (if such a thing were conceivable) to devise yet worse atrocities. He therefore decided to present this summary of what he had written to His Royal Highness the Prince[2] to implore him to do everything in his power to persuade His Majesty to frustrate the plans of these men. It seemed to him a good idea to have the account printed to enable His Highness to read it more easily. This is the background to the following epitome, or *Short Account.*

2 In this Synopsis Las Casas refers to Emperor Charles V (abdicated 1556) as 'His Majesty' and to his son and heir, the future Philip II, to whom the work is dedicated in the Prologue, as 'His Highness'

PROLOGUE

of Bishop Brother Bartolomé de Las Casas, or Casaus,
to the most high and most mighty Prince of Spain,
our Lord the Prince Philip

Most high and most mighty Lord:

As Divine Providence has ordained that the world shall, for the benefit and proper government of the human race, be divided into kingdoms and peoples and that these shall be ruled by kings, who are (as Homer has it) fathers and shepherds to their people and are, accordingly, the noblest and most virtuous of beings, there is no doubt, nor could there in all reason be any such doubt, but that these kings entertain nothing save that which is morally unimpeachable. It follows that if the commonwealth suffers from some defect, or shortcoming, or evil, the reason can only be that the ruler is unaware of it; once the matter is brought to his notice, he will work with the utmost diligence to set matters right and will not rest content until the evil has been eradicated. This would appear to be the sense of the words of Solomon in the Bible: 'A king that sitteth in the throne of judgement scattereth away all evil with his eyes'.[3] For, granted the innate and natural virtue of the ruler, it follows that the simple knowledge that something is wrong in his kingdom is quite sufficient to ensure that he will see that it is corrected, for he will not tolerate any such evil for a moment longer than it takes him to right it.

Contemplating, therefore (most mighty Lord), as a man with more than fifty[4] years' experience of seeing at first hand the evil and the harm, the losses and diminutions suffered by those great kingdoms, each so vast and so wonderful that it would be more appropriate to refer to them as the New World of the Americas –

3 Proverbs 20: 8
4 See Introduction, pp. xviii–xxx

kingdoms granted and entrusted by God and His Church to the Spanish Crown so that they might be properly ruled and governed, converted to the Faith, and tenderly nurtured to full material and spiritual prosperity —[5] I am persuaded that, if Your Highness had been informed of even a few of the excesses which this New World has witnessed, all of them surpassing anything that men hitherto have imagined even in their wildest dreams, Your Highness would not have delayed for even one moment before entreating His Majesty to prevent any repetition of the atrocities which go under the name of 'conquests': excesses which, if no move is made to stop them, will be committed time and again, and which (given that the indigenous peoples of the region are naturally so gentle, so peace-loving, so humble and so docile) are of themselves iniquitous, tyrannical, contrary to natural, canon, and civil law, and are deemed wicked and are condemned and proscribed by all such legal codes. I therefore concluded that it would constitute a criminal neglect of my duty to remain silent about the enormous loss of life as well as the infinite number of human souls despatched to Hell in the course of such 'conquests', and so resolved to publish an account of a few such outrages (and they can be only a few out of the countless number of such incidents that I could relate) in order to make that account the more accessible to Your Highness.

Thus it was that, when the then bishop of Cartagena and tutor to your Highness, the archbishop of Toledo,[6] asked me for a copy of my *Account*, I duly gave him one and this he presented to Your Highness. But Your Highness has been fully occupied with journeys, by land and sea, as well as other pressing royal

5 The reference is to the Bulls of Donation of 1493 by the terms of which Pope Alexander VI conceded to Ferdinand and Isabella sovereignty over the Americas in exchange for an obligation to convert their inhabitants to Christianity. See Introduction, p. xvi

6 Juan Martínez de Silíceo, a rare bird indeed in mid-sixteenth-century Spain. The son of a rural labourer, he rose to be a philosophy professor at the university of Salamanca, tutor-confessor to Prince Philip, bishop of Cartagena (1540), and archbishop of Toledo (1546)

business,[7] and it may well be that Your Highness has never found the time to read the *Account*, or has perhaps allowed it to slip to the back of your mind. Meanwhile, the boldness and the unreason of those who count it as nothing to drench the Americas in human blood and to dispossess the people who are the natural masters and dwellers in those vast and marvellous kingdoms, killing a thousand million of them, and stealing treasures beyond compare, grow by the day, and, masquerading under false colours, they do everything within their power to obtain further licence to continue their conquests (licence that cannot be granted without infringing natural and divine law and thereby conniving at the gravest of mortal sins, worthy of the most terrible and everlasting punishment). I therefore determined to present Your Highness with this *Short Account*, which is but a brief digest of the many and various outrages and depredations which could and should be recorded. I implore Your Highness to accept it and to read it in that spirit of clemency and royal benevolence with which Your Highness traditionally approaches the works of those of Your Highness's subjects and servants whose only desire is to serve the public good and the interests of the Crown. It is my fervent hope that, once Your Highness perceives the extent of the injustices suffered by these innocent peoples and the way in which they are being destroyed and crushed underfoot, unjustly and for no other reason than to satisfy the greed and ambition of those whose purpose it is to commit such wicked atrocities, Your Highness will see fit to beg and entreat His Majesty to refuse all those who seek royal licence for such evil and detestable ventures, and to put a stop once and for all to their infernal clamour in such a way that nobody will henceforth dare to make such a request nor even to mention ventures of this kind.

This, Your Royal Highness, is a matter on which action is

7 This would appear to be a reference to Philip's visit to the Netherlands in 1549, the last time he was ever to leave the Iberian Peninsula

both urgent and necessary if God is to continue to watch over the Crown of Castile and ensure its future well-being and prosperity, both spiritual and temporal. Amen.

[PREFACE]

The Americas were discovered in 1492, and the first Christian settlements established by the Spanish the following year. It is accordingly forty-nine years now since Spaniards began arriving in numbers in this part of the world.[8] They first settled the large and fertile island of Hispaniola, which boasts six hundred leagues of coastline and is surrounded by a great many other large islands, all of them, as I saw for myself, with as high a native population as anywhere on earth.[9] Of the coast of the mainland, which, at its nearest point, is a little over two hundred and fifty leagues from Hispaniola, more than ten thousand leagues had been explored by 1541, and more are being discovered every day. This coastline, too, was swarming with people and it would seem, if we are to judge by those areas so far explored, that the Almighty selected this part of the world as home to the greater part of the human race.

God made all the peoples of this area, many and varied as they are, as open and as innocent as can be imagined. The simplest people in the world — unassuming, long-suffering, unassertive, and submissive — they are without malice or guile, and are utterly faithful and obedient both to their own native lords and

8 The *Short Account* was written in 1542; see Introduction, p. xv
9 The island of Hispaniola, comprising today Haiti and the Dominican Republic, is, at its most extensive, some 400 miles from west to east and covers an area of nearly 30,000 square miles. The Spanish league (*legua*) was calculated as one twenty-fifth of a degree of latitude measured on the earth's surface, or about 2.6 miles (compare the 'maritime' or 'mariners'' league equal to three minutes or one twentieth of a degree of latitude). In the absence of reliable means of measuring distances accurately, a day's journey on horseback was often calculated, whatever the terrain, at seven *leguas* (Hernán Cortés, *Letters from Mexico*, translated by Anthony Pagden (London: OUP, 1972, 2nd ed., New Haven and London: Yale U.P., 1986, p. 529)

to the Spaniards in whose service they now find themselves. Never quarrelsome or belligerent or boisterous, they harbour no grudges and do not seek to settle old scores; indeed, the notions of revenge, rancour, and hatred are quite foreign to them. At the same time, they are among the least robust of human beings: their delicate constitutions make them unable to withstand hard work or suffering and render them liable to succumb to almost any illness, no matter how mild. Even the common people are no tougher than princes or than other Europeans born with a silver spoon in their mouths and who spend their lives shielded from the rigours of the outside world. They are also among the poorest people on the face of the earth; they own next to nothing and have no urge to acquire material possessions. As a result they are neither ambitious nor greedy, and are totally uninterested in worldly power. Their diet is every bit as poor and as monotonous, in quantity and in kind, as that enjoyed by the Desert Fathers. Most of them go naked, save for a loincloth to cover their modesty; at best they may wrap themselves in a piece of cotton material a yard or two square. Most sleep on matting, although a few possess a kind of hanging net, known in the language of Hispaniola as a hammock.[10] They are innocent and pure in mind and have a lively intelligence, all of which makes them particularly receptive to learning and understanding the truths of our Catholic faith and to being instructed in virtue; indeed, God has invested them with fewer impediments in this regard than any other people on earth. Once they begin to learn of the Christian faith they become so keen to know more, to receive the Sacraments, and to worship God, that the missionaries who instruct them do truly have to be men of exceptional patience and forbearance; and over the years I have time and again met Spanish laymen who have been so struck by the natural goodness that shines through these people that they

10 'Hammock' (*hamaca* in Spanish) is one of a dozen or so words common to a great number of European languages – among them potato, tomato, hurricane – which derive from the Taino language of Santo Domingo

frequently can be heard to exclaim: 'These would be the most blessed people on earth if only they were given the chance to convert to Christianity.'

It was upon these gentle lambs, imbued by the Creator with all the qualities we have mentioned, that from the very first day they clapped eyes on them the Spanish fell like ravening wolves upon the fold, or like tigers and savage lions who have not eaten meat for days. The pattern established at the outset has remained unchanged to this day, and the Spaniards still do nothing save tear the natives to shreds, murder them and inflict upon them untold misery, suffering and distress, tormenting, harrying and persecuting them mercilessly. We shall in due course describe some of the many ingenious methods of torture they have invented and refined for this purpose, but one can get some idea of the effectiveness of their methods from the figures alone. When the Spanish first journeyed there, the indigenous population of the island of Hispaniola stood at some three million; today only two hundred survive. The island of Cuba, which extends for a distance almost as great as that separating Valladolid from Rome, is now to all intents and purposes uninhabited;[11] and two other large, beautiful and fertile islands, Puerto Rico and Jamaica, have been similarly devastated. Not a living soul remains today on any of the islands of the Bahamas, which lie to the north of Hispaniola and Cuba, even though every single one of the sixty or so islands in the group, as well as those known as the Isles of Giants and others in the area, both large and small, is more fertile and more beautiful than the Royal Gardens in Seville and the climate is as healthy as anywhere on earth.[12] The native population, which once numbered some five hundred thousand, was wiped out by forcible expatriation to the island of Hispaniola, a policy adopted by the Spaniards in an endeavour

11 The maximum east–west extent of Cuba is approximately 700 miles; the distance from Valladolid to Rome some 750

12 The Royal Gardens (*Huerta del Rey*) were an extensive pleasure ground lying outside the Seville city walls

to make up losses among the indigenous population of that island. One God-fearing individual was moved to mount an expedition to seek out those who had escaped the Spanish trawl and were still living in the Bahamas and to save their souls by converting them to Christianity, but, by the end of a search lasting three whole years, they had found only the eleven survivors I saw with my own eyes.[13] A further thirty or so islands in the region of Puerto Rico are also now uninhabited and left to go to rack and ruin as a direct result of the same practices. All these islands, which together must run to over two thousand leagues, are now abandoned and desolate.

On the mainland, we know for sure that our fellow-countrymen have, through their cruelty and wickedness, depopulated and laid waste an area which once boasted more than ten kingdoms, each of them larger in area than the whole of the Iberian Peninsula. The whole region, once teeming with human beings, is now deserted over a distance of more than two thousand leagues: a distance, that is, greater than the journey from Seville to Jerusalem and back again.

At a conservative estimate, the despotic and diabolical behaviour of the Christians has, over the last forty years, led to the unjust and totally unwarranted deaths of more than twelve million souls, women and children among them, and there are grounds for believing my own estimate of more than fifteen million to be nearer the mark.

There are two main ways in which those who have travelled to this part of the world pretending to be Christians have uprooted these pitiful peoples and wiped them from the face of the earth. First, they have waged war on them: unjust, cruel, bloody and tyrannical war. Second, they have murdered anyone and everyone who has shown the slightest sign of resistance, or even of wishing to escape the torment to which they have

---

13 On this expedition, mounted by Pedro de Isla, who would later become a Franciscan friar, see Las Casas, *History of the Indies*, book II, chapter 45

subjected him. This latter policy has been instrumental in suppressing the native leaders, and, indeed, given that the Spaniards normally spare only women and children, it has led to the annihilation of all adult males, whom they habitually subject to the harshest and most iniquitous and brutal slavery that man has ever devised for his fellow-men, treating them, in fact, worse than animals. All the many and infinitely varied ways that have been devised for oppressing these peoples can be seen to flow from one or other of these two diabolical and tyrannical policies.

The reason the Christians have murdered on such a vast scale and killed anyone and everyone in their way is purely and simply greed. They have set out to line their pockets with gold and to amass private fortunes as quickly as possible so that they can then assume a status quite at odds with that into which they were born. Their insatiable greed and overweening ambition know no bounds; the land is fertile and rich, the inhabitants simple, forbearing and submissive. The Spaniards have shown not the slightest consideration for these people, treating them (and I speak from first-hand experience, having been there from the outset) not as brute animals – indeed, I would to God they had done and had shown them the consideration they afford their animals – so much as piles of dung in the middle of the road. They have had as little concern for their souls as for their bodies, all the millions that have perished having gone to their deaths with no knowledge of God and without the benefit of the Sacraments. One fact in all this is widely known and beyond dispute, for even the tyrannical murderers themselves acknowledge the truth of it: the indigenous peoples never did the Europeans any harm whatever; on the contrary, they believed them to have descended from the heavens, at least until they or their fellow-citizens had tasted, at the hands of these oppressors, a diet of robbery, murder, violence, and all other manner of trials and tribulations.

As we have said, the island of Hispaniola was the first to witness the arrival of Europeans and the first to suffer the wholesale slaughter of its people and the devastation and depopulation of the land. It all began with the Europeans taking native women and children both as servants and to satisfy their own base appetites; then, not content with what the local people offered them of their own free will (and all offered as much as they could spare), they started taking for themselves the food the natives contrived to produce by the sweat of their brows, which was in all honesty little enough. Since what a European will consume in a single day normally supports three native households of ten persons each for a whole month, and since the newcomers began to subject the locals to other vexations, assaults, and iniquities, the people began to realize that these men could not, in truth, have descended from the heavens. Some of them started to conceal what food they had, others decided to send their women and children into hiding, and yet others took to the hills to get away from the brutal and ruthless cruelty that was being inflicted on them. The Christians punched them, boxed their ears and flogged them in order to track down the local leaders, and the whole shameful process came to a head when one of the European commanders raped the wife of the paramount chief of the entire island.[14] It was then that the locals began to think up ways of driving the Europeans out of their lands and to take up arms against them. Their weapons, however, were flimsy and ineffective both in attack and in defence (and, indeed, war in the Americas is no more deadly than our jousting,

14 Guarionex; see below, p. 19

or than many European children's games) and, with their horses and swords and lances, the Spaniards easily fended them off, killing them and committing all kind of atrocities against them.

They forced their way into native settlements, slaughtering everyone they found there, including small children, old men, pregnant women, and even women who had just given birth. They hacked them to pieces, slicing open their bellies with their swords as though they were so many sheep herded into a pen. They even laid wagers on whether they could manage to slice a man in two at a stroke, or cut an individual's head from his body, or disembowel him with a single blow of their axes. They grabbed suckling infants by the feet and, ripping them from their mothers' breasts, dashed them headlong against the rocks. Others, laughing and joking all the while, threw them over their shoulders into a river, shouting: 'Wriggle, you little perisher.' They slaughtered anyone and everyone in their path, on occasion running through a mother and her baby with a single thrust of their swords. They spared no one, erecting especially wide gibbets on which they could string their victims up with their feet just off the ground and then burn them alive thirteen at a time, in honour of our Saviour and the twelve Apostles, or tie dry straw to their bodies and set fire to it. Some they chose to keep alive and simply cut their wrists, leaving their hands dangling, saying to them: 'Take this letter' – meaning that their sorry condition would act as a warning to those hiding in the hills. The way they normally dealt with the native leaders and nobles was to tie them to a kind of griddle consisting of sticks resting on pitchforks driven into the ground and then grill them over a slow fire, with the result that they howled in agony and despair as they died a lingering death.

It once happened that I myself witnessed their grilling of four or five local leaders in this fashion (and I believe they had set up two or three other pairs of grills alongside so that they might process other victims at the same time) when the poor creatures' howls came between the Spanish commander and his sleep. He

They spared no one, erecting especially wide gibbets on which they could string their victims up with their feet just off the ground and then burn them alive.

gave orders that the prisoners were to be throttled, but the man in charge of the execution detail, who was more bloodthirsty than the average common hangman (I know his identity and even met some relatives of his in Seville), was loath to cut short his private entertainment by throttling them and so he personally went round ramming wooden bungs into their mouths to stop them making such a racket and deliberately stoked the fire so that they would take just as long to die as he himself chose. I saw all these things for myself and many others besides. And, since all those who could do so took to the hills and mountains in order to escape the clutches of these merciless and inhuman butchers, these mortal enemies of human kind trained hunting dogs to track them down — wild dogs who would savage a native to death as soon as look at him, tearing him to shreds and devouring his flesh as though he were a pig. These dogs wrought havoc among the natives and were responsible for much carnage. And when, as happened on the odd occasion, the locals did kill a European, as, given the enormity of the crimes committed against them, they were in all justice fully entitled to, the Spanish came to an unofficial agreement among themselves that for every European killed one hundred natives would be executed.

THE KINGDOMS OF HISPANIOLA

On Hispaniola there were five main kingdoms, each very extensive and each with its own king; most of the infinite number of local nobles paid allegiance to one or other of these five powerful leaders, although there were a few backwoodsmen who recognized no authority above and beyond their own. One of these kingdoms was called Maguá,[15] with the stress on the last syllable, which means Kingdom of the Plain. This plain is one of the wonders of the world, extending, as it does, for some eighty leagues, right from the southern coast of the island to its northern shore. For the most part it is some five to eight leagues wide and as much as ten in places, and is confined by high mountains on either side. Over thirty thousand streams and rivers flow into it, a dozen of them every bit as big as the Ebro, Duero, and Guadalquivir,[16] and those that come down from the mountains to the west (and there are twenty or twenty-five thousand of them) are rich in alluvial gold. Among those mountains lies the province of Cibao[17] and its mines, famous throughout the region for their very high-quality gold. The king of Cibao was called Guarionex[18] and he had as vassals several extremely powerful local leaders; one of them, for example, had sixteen thousand men under arms and these he placed at the

---

15 See Las Casas, *History of the Indies*, book III, chapter 1
16 The three principal rivers of Spain
17 Columbus called the region 'Cipango' in the belief that it was Japan; see his *History of the Indies*, book I, chapter 60
18 In Las Casas's account – the only one we have – this Guarionex was one of four kings on the island, all of whom perished, together with Francisco Bobadilla and Francisco Roldán, in the shipwreck described below, p. 20. The others were 'Caonabó', 'Behechio', and 'Higuanama'; see Las Casas, *History of the Indies*, book II, chapter 5

service of Guarionex. I met some of these men myself. The king himself was dutiful and virtuous, a man of placid temperament much devoted to the King and Queen of Spain. For a number of years, every householder throughout his realm made, on his orders, an annual gift of a hollow gourd completely filled with gold. The natives of Hispaniola know little of mining techniques and later, when there was less gold available, the king reduced this offering to half a gourd filled with gold. In order to put a stop to the Spaniards' incessant demands for gold, Guarionex suggested that he might better serve the King of Castile by putting a great area of his kingdom under cultivation, especially as his subjects had, as he himself quite correctly asserted, little or no notion of how to mine for gold. Such a plan was feasible, as I can vouch, and the king would have been quite happy to see it put into effect. The area involved would have stretched from Isabela, the site of the first European settlement on the island, as far as Santo Domingo, some fifty or more leagues distant, and it would easily have produced an annual income of over three million *castilians*[19] and, had such a scheme been put into effect, it would have led to the establishment of fifty or more cities on the island, every one of them as large as Seville.[20]

The wicked European commanders rewarded this good and great man by dishonouring him when one of their number[21] took and raped his wife. To this the king could easily have reacted by biding his time and gathering an army to exact revenge, but he elected instead to abdicate and go into voluntary exile, alone, to an area called Ciguayos, where the powerful local leader was one of his vassals.[22] Once the Europeans realized he had gone, there was no chance of keeping his whereabouts secret, and they got up an army and attacked the local leader under whose

---

19 The *castilian* was a gold coin worth some 480 *maravedís* and weighing 1.6 ounces
20 The population of Seville has been estimated at between sixty and seventy thousand in 1500 and approximately one hundred thousand in 1565
21 Francisco Roldán, one of the companions of Columbus
22 Mayonabex. On his death, see Las Casas, *History of the Indies*, book I, chapter 123

protection the king was sheltering. The carnage was terrible and, eventually, they tracked down the fugitive, took him prisoner, put him in chains and shackles and bundled him on to a ship bound for Castile, only for him to perish, along with many Spaniards, when the ship was lost at sea.[23] A fortune in gold sank beneath the waves that day, among the cargo being the Great Nugget, as big as a loaf of bread[24] and weighing three thousand six hundred *castilians*. In this way, God passed judgement on the great iniquities committed by the Spanish.

Another of these original kingdoms occupied the northern end of the plain where the royal harbour is today. Known as Marién, it was a rich region, larger than Portugal, although a good deal more fertile and far better suited to human habitation, criss-crossed as it is by several mighty mountain ranges and seamed with productive gold and copper mines. The king of this area was called Guacanagarí, with the stress on the last syllable, and he numbered among his vassals many men of high standing, several of whom I knew personally. This was the first place where the old Admiral[25] who discovered the New World first landed and was received on that occasion by this Guacanagarí, as were all his crew, with the greatest kindness and humanity imaginable. As Columbus himself told me, it was there that the Admiral's own ship was lost[26] and he and his men were as graciously treated and looked after as if they had been back home and were all part of the same close family. Guacanagarí himself died up in the mountains, broken and destitute, after he had fled to escape the massacres and the cruelty inflicted by the Spaniards, and all the other local leaders who owed allegiance to Guacanagarí perished as a direct result of the despotism and

23 In 1502
24 The term used by Las Casas for a loaf of bread (*hogaza*) normally referred at this time to the largest of loaves in common use, round in shape and weighing more than two pounds. By this calculation, the Great Nugget would have weighed over three hundredweight (but see Introduction, pp. xxxi–xxxii)
25 Christopher Columbus
26 Columbus's flagship, the *Santa María*, was lost on Christmas Day 1492

slavery to which they were subjected and which I shall in due course set out in detail.

The third of these kingdoms was the sovereign state of Maguana, another strikingly beautiful and fertile area and one which enjoyed the healthiest of climates. It is this area that nowadays produces the best sugar on the whole island. The king, Caonabó, who outdid all others in strength, majesty of bearing and court ceremonial, was captured by an underhand trick and taken from his own house. He was put on board one of the Spanish ships bound for Castile; but the Almighty determined not to allow this act of duplicity and injustice to pass unnoticed and, that night, sent a violent storm in which all six of the ships, still in harbour and on the very point of setting sail, sank with the loss of all hands. Caonabó, shackled and chained as he was, perished along with them.[27] He had three or four brothers, all of them as valorous and as brave as he was himself, and, when they saw how their brother and lord had unjustly been taken prisoner and learned of the devastation and the massacres the Europeans had set in train in other parts of the island, they took up arms, determined, all the more so when they got wind of their brother's death, to attack the Europeans and take revenge upon them. But the Christians, several of whom were on horseback (and the horse is the deadliest weapon imaginable against these people), attacked instead, slaughtering them to such effect that they destroyed and depopulated a good half of the kingdom.

The fourth kingdom was known as Xaraguá, and was really the heart and core of the whole island. In no other part of the island was the language as refined as here nor the court discourse as cultivated; nowhere else were the people of such quality and breeding, the leading families as numerous and as liberal – and this kingdom boasted many nobles and great lords – nor the inhabitants as handsome and easy on the eye. Chief among them

27 On the capture of Caonabó by Alonso de Hojeda and his subsequent loss at sea, see Las Casas, *History of the Indies*, book I, chapter 102

were the king, Behechio,[28] and his sister, Anacaona, both of whom rendered great service to the Spanish Crown and gave every assistance to the European settlers, on occasion even saving their lives; after Behechio's death, Anacaona ruled in his stead. Over three hundred local dignitaries were summoned to welcome the then governor of the island[29] when he paid a visit to the kingdom with sixty horse and a further three hundred men on foot (the horsemen alone were sufficient in number to ravage not only the whole island but the mainland as well). The governor duped the unsuspecting leaders of this welcoming party into gathering in a building made of straw and then ordered his men to set fire to it and burn them alive. All the others were massacred, either run through by lances or put to the sword. As a mark of respect and out of deference to her rank, Queen Anacaona was hanged. When one or two Spaniards tried to save some of the children, either because they genuinely pitied them or perhaps because they wanted them for themselves, and swung them up behind them on to their horses, one of their compatriots rode up behind and ran them through with his lance. Yet another member of the governor's party galloped about cutting the legs off all the children as they lay sprawling on the ground. The governor even decreed that those who made their way to a small island some eight leagues distant in order to escape this bestial cruelty should be condemned to slavery because they had fled the carnage.

The fifth kingdom was known as Higuey and its queen, a lady already advanced in years, went by the name of Higuanama.[30]

28 See above, p. 18, n. 18
29 Presumably Nicolás de Ovando (1451–1511), who was made governor of the Americas in 1501 and reached Hispaniola in April of the following year. According to his own account, Las Casas arrived in the Antilles in the same fleet; see Introduction, p. xix. Here, as throughout the *Short Account*, Las Casas refrains from identifying individuals by name (see Introduction, p. xl). For an exception see below, p. 77, n. 97
30 See above, p. 18, n. 18. In book I of his *History of the Indies*, chapter 100, Las Casas refers to Higuanama as a 'king' but in book II, chapter 8, calls her 'an old and great queen'

They strung her up and I saw with my own eyes how the Spaniards burned countless local inhabitants alive or hacked them to pieces, or devised novel ways of torturing them to death, enslaving those they took alive. Indeed, they invented so many new methods of murder that it would be quite impossible to set them all down on paper and, however hard one tried to chronicle them, one could probably never list a thousandth part of what actually took place. All I can say is that I know it to be an incontrovertible fact and do here so swear before Almighty God, that the local peoples never gave the Spanish any cause whatever for the injury and injustice that was done to them in these campaigns. On the contrary, they behaved as honourably as might the inmates of a well-run monastery, and for this they were robbed and massacred, and even those who escaped death on this occasion found themselves condemned to a lifetime of captivity and slavery. I would go further. It is my firm belief that not a single native of the island committed a capital offence, as defined in law, against the Spanish while all this time the natives themselves were being savaged and murdered. Despite the enormous provocation, very few of the natives, I hazard, were guilty of even those sins which do not lie within the ambit of human law but are properly the province of God, such as hatred and anger, or the thirst for revenge against those who committed such enormities upon them. It is my own experience of these peoples, gained over many years, that they are no more given to impetuous actions or to harbouring thoughts of retribution than are boys of ten or twelve years of age. I know beyond any shadow of a doubt that they had, from the very beginning, every right to wage war on the Europeans, while the Europeans never had just cause for waging war on the local peoples. The actions of the Europeans, throughout the New World, were without exception wicked and unjust: worse, in fact, than the blackest kind of tyranny.

After the fighting was over and all the men had been killed, the surviving natives – usually, that is, the young boys, the women, and the children – were shared out between the victors. One got thirty, another forty, a third as many as a hundred or even twice that number; everything depended on how far one was in the good books of the despot who went by the title of governor. The pretext under which the victims were parcelled out in this way was that their new masters would then be in a position to teach them the truths of the Christian faith; and thus it came about that a host of cruel, grasping and wicked men, almost all of them pig-ignorant, were put in charge of these poor souls. And they discharged this duty by sending the men down the mines, where working conditions were appalling, to dig for gold, and putting the women to labour in the fields and on their master's estates, to till the soil and raise the crops, properly a task only for the toughest and strongest of men. Both women and men were given only wild grasses to eat and other unnutritious foodstuffs. The mothers of young children promptly saw their milk dry up and their babies die; and, with the women and the men separated and never seeing each other, no new children were born. The men died down the mines from overwork and starvation, and the same was true of the women who perished out on the estates. The islanders, previously so numerous, began to die out as would any nation subjected to such appalling treatment.[31] For example, they were made to carry burdens of three and four *arrobas*[32] for distances of up to a hundred or even two hundred leagues, and were forced to carry their Christian masters in hammocks, which are like nets slung from the shoulders of the bearers. In short, they were treated as beasts of

31 Figures for the pre-contact population of the Antilles are necessarily wildly approximate. The highest is about eight million; the lowest – and, because it is based on the potential agricultural yield of the land, the most reliable – is around half a million. The total population of the islands when the *Short Account* was written did not exceed three hundred thousand. By the middle of the seventeeth century, the Arawak were virtually extinct.

32 The *arroba*, in origin an Arabic term, was widely used throughout the Spanish empire as a measure, both of weight (roughly 25 pounds) and of dry capacity (roughly 15 litres), though its precise value varied regionally

burden and developed huge sores on their shoulders and backs as happens with animals made to carry excessive loads. And this is not to mention the floggings, beatings, thrashings, punches, curses and countless other vexations and cruelties to which they were routinely subjected and to which no chronicle could ever do justice nor any reader respond save with horror and disbelief.

It is of note that all these island territories began to go to the dogs once news arrived of the death of our most gracious Queen Isabella, who departed this life in 1504.[33] Up to then, only a small number of provinces had been destroyed through unjust military action, not the whole area, and news of even this partial destruction had by and large been kept from the Queen, because, she – may her soul rest in peace – took a close personal interest in the physical and spiritual welfare of the native peoples, as those of us who lived through those years and saw examples of it with our own eyes can attest. There is one other general rule in all this, and it is that, wherever the Spaniards set foot, right throughout the Americas, they subjected the native inhabitants to the cruelties of which we have spoken, killing these poor and innocent people, tyrannizing them, and oppressing them in the most abominable fashion. The longer they spent in the region the more ingenious were the torments, each crueller than the last, that they inflicted on their victims, as God finally abandoned them and left them to plummet headlong into a life of full-time crime and wickedness.

33 This is a pious exaggeration. Yet it was Queen Isabella (died Medina del Campo, Old Castile, 26 November 1504) who, in 1495, had prevented Columbus from selling Amerindians as slaves and who, in 1501, instructed Ovando that she wished the inhabitants of Hispaniola 'to be well treated as our subjects and our vassals'; see Anthony Pagden, *The Fall of Natural Man: The American Indians and the Origins of Comparative Ethnology,* second edition (Cambridge: Cambridge University Press, 1986), pp. 41–2

THE ISLANDS OF PUERTO RICO AND
JAMAICA

In 1509, the Spanish, with the same purpose in mind as they had when they landed on Hispaniola, found their way to the two verdant islands of Puerto Rico and Jamaica, both of them lands flowing with milk and honey.[34] Here they perpetrated the same outrages and committed the same crimes as before, devising yet further refinements of cruelty, murdering the native people, burning and roasting them alive, throwing them to wild dogs[35] and then oppressing, tormenting and plaguing them with toil down the mines and elsewhere, and so once again killing off these poor innocents to such effect that where the native population of the two islands was certainly over six hundred thousand (and I personally reckon it at more than a million) fewer than two hundred survive on each of the two islands, all the others having perished without ever learning the truths of the Christian religion and without the benefit of the Sacraments.

34 These expeditions of Juan Ponce de León to Puerto Rico and Juan de Esquivel to Jamaica are discussed at greater length in Las Casas, *History of the Indies*, book II, chapters 46-55

35 Spanish mastiffs proved one of the most feared and most effective weapons of the conquest. The only dogs known to the indigenous inhabitants of the Antilles were the ancestors of the modern Chihuahua, very small and edible

CUBA

In 1511 the Spanish set foot on Cuba. This island, which, as we have said, stretched for a distance as great as that which separates Valladolid from Rome,[36] was home to a great many people. The Spanish set about treating them all in the manner we have already described, only even more cruelly. A number of extraordinary incidents took place here. One of the leading local lords, a cacique[37] who went by the name of Hatuey, had fled to the island from Hispaniola with many of his people in order to escape the miseries that arose from the inhuman treatment meted out to the natives of that island by the Spanish. When he heard that the Christians had now switched their attention to Cuba, he gathered most if not all his people about him and addressed them, saying: 'You know that rumour has it that the Christians are coming to this island, and you already know what they have done to the lord so-and-so and so-and-so and so-and-so. What they did on Haiti (which is another name for Hispaniola) they will do again here. Does any of you know why it is that they behave in this way?' And when they answered him: 'No, unless it be that they are innately cruel and evil', he replied: 'It is not simply that. They have a God whom they worship and adore, and it is in order to get that God from us so that they can worship Him that they conquer us and kill us.' He had beside him, as he spoke, a basket filled with gold jewellery and he said:

36 See above, p. 11. The Cuba expedition was under the command of Diego Velázquez; see Introduction, p. xxi
37 The Arawak term *cacique* simply designated a tribal leader, but it came to be used by the Spanish administration all over the Americas to describe Amerindian chieftains who were believed to be inferior in rank to 'kings' and 'princes' (*principales*) and who were frequently employed as tax-gatherers

'Here is the God of the Christians. If you agree, we will do *areitos* (which is their word for certain kinds of traditional dance) in honour of this God and it may be that we shall please Him and He will order the Christians to leave us unharmed.' They all shouted: 'So be it, so be it.' And after they had danced before this god until they were dropping from exhaustion, the lord Hatuey addressed them once again, saying: 'Mark you: if we keep this God about us, they will kill us in order to get their hands on Him. Let us throw Him into this river.' And they were all agreed, and so they threw the god into a great river nearby.

This same cacique and lord knew the Spaniards and their ways only too well and he fled from them once they arrived on the island of Cuba, only resorting to outright resistance when they actually tracked him down. But, eventually, he was captured and, although his only crime was that he had tried to escape the clutches of these cruel and iniquitous monsters because he knew only too well that they were out to kill him and that, if he did not defend himself, they would hound him and all his people to death, the Spaniards' verdict was that he should be burned alive. Once he was tied to the stake, a Franciscan friar who was present, a saintly man,[38] told him as much as he could in the short time permitted by his executioners about the Lord and about our Christian faith, all of which was new to him. The friar told him that, if he would only believe what he was now hearing, he would go to Heaven there to enjoy glory and eternal rest, but that, if he would not, he would be consigned to Hell, where he would endure everlasting pain and torment. The lord Hatuey thought for a short while and then asked the friar whether Christians went to Heaven. When the reply came that good ones do, he retorted, without need for further reflection, that, if that was the case, then he chose to go to Hell to ensure that he would never again have to clap eyes on those cruel

38 Details of this story may be found in Las Casas, *History of the Indies*, book III, chapters 21 and 25

brutes. This is just one example of the reputation and honour that our Lord and our Christian faith have earned as a result of the actions of those 'Christians' who have sailed to the Americas.

On one occasion, when the locals had come some ten leagues out from a large settlement in order to receive us and regale us with victuals and other gifts, and had given us loaves and fishes and any other foodstuffs they could provide, the Christians were suddenly inspired by the Devil and, without the slightest provocation, butchered, before my eyes, some three thousand souls – men, women and children – as they sat there in front of us. I saw that day atrocities more terrible than any living man has ever seen nor ever thought to see.

Only a few days later, with the whole island still reeling at news of this massacre and acting on assurances I obtained from our commander,[39] I sent messages to all the nobles of Havana province, as they had all heard of me and knew I could be trusted, assuring them that there was no reason to be afraid and that no harm would befall them if they came to meet us. When we arrived in the province, twenty-one local lords and caciques did indeed make up a welcoming party. But the commander immediately seized them, thereby breaking the promise I had given, and was all for burning them alive the very next day, saying that there was nothing wrong with doing so because, given time, they were bound to do something that merited such punishment. I had a difficult job keeping them from the stake, but in the end they did all make good their escape.[40]

Once all the inhabitants of this island found themselves in the same hopeless predicament as had those on Hispaniola – that is, they were either enslaved or foully murdered – some began to

39 Pánfilo de Narváez (?1480–1528). He had participated with Diego Velázquez in the conquest of Cuba and in 1520 led an army to Mexico in an unsuccessful attempt to wrest control of the country from Hernán Cortés (see below, p. 48). In 1527 he captained an ill-fated expedition to Florida and the following year was the first European to land on the coast of what is today Texas

40 Details of the massacre of Caonao are given at greater length in Las Casas, *History of the Indies*, book III, chapters 29–30

flee into the hills while others were in such despair that they took their own lives. Men and women hanged themselves and even strung up their own children. As a direct result of the barbarity of one Spaniard (a man I knew personally) more than two hundred locals committed suicide, countless thousands in all dying in this way.

There was one royal official on the island who, when he was allotted three hundred natives, worked them so hard that, at the end of three months, only thirty – that is to say, just one tenth of the original number – were still alive, the other two hundred and seventy having perished down the mines. Later, he received another consignment of much the same number, or even more, and he saw them off, too. The more he received, the more he killed, until eventually he himself died and the Devil took his soul.

During the three or four months I was there, more than seven thousand children died of hunger, after their parents had been shipped off to the mines, and I saw many other horrors also.

It was later decided to hunt down the natives who had fled into the mountains, and the subsequent hunting parties were responsible for carnage beyond belief. Thus it was that the whole of the island was devastated and depopulated, and it now affords, as we discovered on a recent visit, a moving and heart-rending spectacle, transformed, as it has been, into one vast, barren wasteland.

THE MAINLAND

It was in 1514 that a governor landed on the Mainland.[41] This man, who descended on the region like the wrath of God, was the cruellest of tyrants, totally devoid as he was of any feelings of mercy or even of common sense. He was determined to settle the whole area with Spaniards. The Mainland had seen its share of despots before, who had pillaged and murdered and alienated the local people, but their depredations and iniquities had so far been confined to the coastal areas. This individual, however, outstripped all his predecessors, transcending in cruelty even those that had ravaged the islands, and his devilish deeds surpassed all the abominations that had taken place before his arrival. Nor did he confine his attentions to the coastal area, but cut great swathes through the interior, driving the locals out, killing left, right and centre, and despatching everyone he encountered to Hell. He devastated the land for many leagues north of Darién right up to and including the kingdom and provinces of Nicaragua – a distance of more than five hundred leagues over some of the most fertile and densely populated areas that are to be found anywhere in the known world. It was a region in which there lived many great lords, and where there were countless large cities. Nowhere on the face of the earth had such an enormous wealth of gold been discovered, for, although the island of Hispaniola had filled Spain to over-flowing with gold, and gold of the highest quality, this had all to be extracted from the bowels of the earth by the sweat

41 Pedro Arias de Ávila, or Pedrarias Dávila; see Cortés, *Letters from Mexico*, pp. 513–14. The Mainland (*Tierra Firme*) was the name given to northern South America and southern Central America, and was the area referred to by the English as the 'Spanish Main'

of natives who toiled down the mines and, as we have noted, perished there.

This governor and his men dreamed up new ways of tormenting the native population and whole new techniques for torturing them in order to force them to reveal the whereabouts of their gold and to hand it over. A Franciscan friar, Francisco de San Román, witnessed at first hand an expedition, mounted by the governor and led by one of his right-hand men to wipe out the natives and rob them of everything they possessed. His report suggests that this expedition alone resulted in the deaths of over forty thousand natives, who were variously put to the sword, burned alive, thrown to wild dogs, or subjected to torture of one form or another.

From the very beginning, Spanish policy towards the New World has been characterized by blindness of the most pernicious kind: even while the various ordinances and decrees governing the treatment of the native peoples have continued to maintain that conversion and the saving of souls has first priority, this is belied by what has actually been happening on the ground. The gulf that yawns between theory and practice has meant that, in fact, the local people have been presented with an ultimatum: either they adopt the Christian religion and swear allegiance to the Crown of Castile, or they will find themselves faced with military action in which no quarter will be given and they will be cut down or taken prisoner. It is as though the Son of God, who gave His life for every living soul, when He instructed His followers with the words: 'Go ye therefore, and teach all nations',[42] intended heathens, living in peace and tranquillity in their own lands, to be confronted with a demand that they convert on the spot, without their ever hearing the Word or having Christian doctrine explained to them; and that, should they show any reluctance to do so and to swear allegiance to a king they have never heard of nor clapped eyes on, and whose

42 Matthew 28: 19, a text much cited in justification of missionary work

subjects and ambassadors prove to be cruel, pitiless and blood-thirsty tyrants, they should immediately surrender all their worldly goods and lose all rights to their land, their freedom, their womenfolk, their children and their lives. Such a notion is as absurd as it is stupid and should be treated with the disrespect, scorn and contempt it so amply deserves. This wicked wretch of a governor was accordingly under instructions to ensure that the terms of this government legislation were made known to the native population, as though by doing this one could justify the absurdity, unreasonableness and injustice of the terms them-selves;[43] what he did in practice, whenever he or the bandits in his employ learned that there was gold in a particular town or village, was to get his gang of robbers to make their way there at dead of night, when the inhabitants were all in bed and sound asleep and, once they got within, say, half a league of the town itself, to read out the terms of this edict, proclaiming (and only to themselves): 'Leaders and citizens of such-and-such a town of this Mainland. Be it known to you that there is one true God, one Pope, and one King of Castile who is the rightful owner of all these lands. You are hereby summoned to pay allegiance, etc. Should you fail to do so, take notice that we shall make just war upon you, and your lives and liberty will be forfeit, etc.' Then, in the early hours of the morning, when the poor people were still innocently abed with their wives and their children, they would irrupt into the town, setting fire to the houses, which were commonly of straw, and burning the women and children alive and often the men, too, before the poor wretches realized what was happening. They would slaughter the people with impunity and those they took alive they either tortured to death in an attempt to get them to tell of other towns where there might be gold or of the whereabouts of more gold in their own town, or else they branded them as slaves. Once the fires had died down or gone out, they conducted a house-to-house search

43 The legislation referred to is the *Requerimiento* of 1513; see Introduction, pp. xxiv–xxv

for gold. This was how this wicked man and his evil followers spent their waking hours from 1514 until 1521 or 1522: amassing a huge fortune (over and above, that is, his stipend as Captain General) by sending five or six or more of his close associates on raiding parties such as this and then taking his share of all the gold, pearls and jewels they plundered as well as of the slaves they took. Other Crown servants behaved in much the same fashion, each of them releasing as many men as he could spare to participate in these raids; even the first bishop of the kingdom[44] sent his underlings so that he, too, could get his hands on a share of the loot. My own conservative estimate of the total value of the gold stolen from that kingdom during these few years is that it amounted to more than a million *castilians*, and of those only some three thousand ever found their way into the royal coffers. Over eight hundred thousand souls perished as a direct result of operations such as these. The villains who succeeded the butcher of whom we have been speaking as governors of the province right up until 1533 either massacred the survivors or else turned a blind eye when others did, the few who were not slaughtered being taken prisoner and later dying in the slavery to which they were reduced after the actual fighting had come to an end.

One could list a whole host of other atrocities perpetrated by this man or to which he turned a blind eye. When, for example, one of the local lords or caciques made him an outright gift of nine thousand *castilians*, either because he wanted to or (more plausibly) because he was in terror of the Spaniards, they seized him and, tying him in a sitting position to a stake set in the ground, lit a fire under his outstretched feet to induce him to hand over yet more gold. He sent home for a further three thousand *castilians*, but they were still not satisfied and recommenced the torture. When he produced no further gold, either

---

44 Fray Juan Cabedo (or Quevedo); see Las Casas, *History of the Indies*, book III, chapter 59

because he had no more or because he chose not to, they car
on until all the marrow ran out through the soles of his feet and
he died. And this is but one of countless examples of murder and
torture inflicted on the natives in this relentless search for gold.

On another occasion a troop of soldiers on a pillaging expedition happened upon a mountain region where a large number of
natives had sought refuge from the reign of terror the Christians
were conducting in their towns and villages. Taking the fugitives
by surprise, they carried off seventy or eighty women and young
girls, killing at the same time as many of the men as they could.
The following day, the survivors regrouped and, sick with
worry about their wives and daughters, set off in pursuit of the
soldiers. Finding themselves hard-pressed, and loath to allow
their pace to slacken, the soldiers stuck their swords into the
guts of the women and the young girls, massacring every single
one of them. The native men, beside themselves with grief and
tearing at their own flesh, shouted after them, saying: 'Oh,
wicked men! Oh, cruel Christians! You kill *iras*!' The word *ira* is
the local term for women, and what they meant by shouting in
this fashion was: 'Killing women is a cruel abomination, and
clear proof that you are brutes and no better than wild beasts.'[45]

Some ten or fifteen leagues from Panama lived a great lord
who went by the name of Paris.[46] He had amassed gold in great
quantity and, when a party of Europeans arrived in his territory,
he received them as long-lost brothers and made the captain of
the party a gift of fifty thousand *castilians*. It seemed to the
captain and his men that someone who could make an unsolicited
gift of that magnitude must be very rich indeed and, gold being
the reason for their presence in the first place, they made a
pretence of departing, only to return at the dead of night when
the place was undefended. They set fire to the buildings, killing

45 Las Casas may have intended a pun here with the Spanish word *ira* ('anger'):
'You murder anger'
46 In the *History of the Indies*, book II, chapter 120, the land is variously given as
'Pariza', 'Paris' and 'Pariba', and its cacique as Cutara

and burning many of the locals, and stealing a further fifty or sixty thousand *castilians*. The local lord himself escaped with his life and, mustering as many men as he could, set off after the soldiers; in two or three days he had caught up with them and their loot of a hundred and thirty or a hundred and forty thousand *castilians*.[47] He and his men set about them valiantly, killing fifty of them, severely wounding many others, putting them to flight and making off with all the gold. Later, a large band of Christians mounted an attack on this lord, butchering him along with vast numbers of his people and taking all the survivors into slavery, where they duly perished, so that today not a trace remains of what was previously a community with dominion over an area of some thirty leagues. So widespread was the ruin and carnage inflicted by this wicked Spanish governor throughout the region that no accurate record can now be compiled and today the whole area lies abandoned and deserted.

47 The numerical inconsistency is in the original

This same tyrant[48] set out in 1522 or 1523 – a black date for the inhabitants of the area – to add to his fiefdom the very fertile province of Nicaragua. It would be impossible to express in words the beauty and fertility of this region, its healthy climate and the prosperity of its many people. The sheer number and size of the towns in the area was truly astonishing: it was often three and four leagues from one end of a town to the other, and the quality and abundance of the local produce was sufficient to support a huge population. The terrain here is flat and level and there are no mountains for the locals to hide in; it is also quite delightful and the people were extremely reluctant to leave. So they stayed and put up as best they might with persecution by the soldiers, with the atrocities they committed, and the slavery they inflicted upon them. These people are also naturally gentle and unaggressive. The despot himself and his tyrannical companions proceeded to wreck this region just as they had wrecked others: they indulged in the same outrages, the same wanton destruction, the same wholesale slaughter, the same atrocities as they had elsewhere; indeed, it is beyond human capacity to compile an accurate log of the murder, cruelty, false imprisonment and other crimes they committed. He sent fifty men on horseback who proceeded to annihilate the entire population of an area greater than the county of Roussillon,[49] sparing not a single man or woman, old man or child, and this they did on the flimsiest of pretexts, accusing their victims of not coming

48 Pedrarias Dávila; see above p. 31, n. 41
49 The county of Roussillon, astride the Eastern Pyrenees with its capital at Perpignan

quickly enough when they were summoned, or of not having brought enough *cargas*[50] of maize (which is to the region what wheat is to Europe), or of not surrendering sufficient of their kinsmen as slaves either to the governor himself or to one or another of his henchmen. These men were driven by the Devil and not a single native managed to escape, what with the land being as flat as it was and the Spaniards having horses.

He sent expeditionary forces (that is, raiding parties) to other provinces and permitted his accomplices to take off as slaves as many of these harmless and peace-loving natives as they chose. They would chain their prisoners together so that none could slip the load of three *arrobas*[51] which he or she was forced to carry. On one of these occasions – and there were many such – of the four thousand natives who began the journey loaded down in this fashion not even six ever saw their homeland again, all the others being left by the roadside where they fell. And when a native bearer flagged and became utterly debilitated and wearied by the enormous burden he was expected to carry and the shortage of food and lack of rest, they cut his head from his shoulders so they would not have to break the chains that held the line of prisoners together, and his head would fall to one side of the baggage train and his trunk to the other. You can imagine what effect this had upon his companions in misery. And, in time, as they came to realize that none of their people ever returned from pilgrimages of this kind, the impressed natives would set out on such a trip with tears running down their cheeks, sighing and bemoaning their fate, saying: 'These are the roads we travelled to go and offer to work for the Christians, and, however hard the work, we thought to return in time to our homes and to our wives and children. That expectation is now a thing of the past, and we know that this trip will be our last.'

---

50 The Spanish term *carga*, generally denoting the maximum quantity a single man could carry at any one time, was also used more narrowly in Castile as a measure of cereals, equal to four *fanegas* or just over six bushels

51 See above, p. 24, n. 32

On one occasion the governor decided on a re-allocation of slaves, either on a whim or (as some say) because he wanted to remove them from a number of his companions with whom he was no longer on good terms and share them out among his latest cronies. As a result of this upheaval, the natives did not get a chance to sow some of the fields, and consequently there was not enough grain to go round. The Christians seized all the maize the locals had grown for themselves and their own families and, as a consequence, some twenty or thirty thousand natives died of hunger, some mothers even killing their own children and eating them.

As we have said, all the towns of the region stood amid fertile lands of their own. Each of the settlers took up residence in the town allotted to him (or *encommended* to him as the legal phrase has it),[52] put the inhabitants to work for him, stole their already scarce foodstuffs for himself and took over the lands owned and worked by the natives and on which they traditionally grew their own produce. The settler would treat the whole of the native population – dignitaries, old men, women and children – as members of his household and, as such, make them labour night and day in his own interests, without any rest whatever; even the small children, as soon as they could stand, were made to do as much as they could, and more. Thus have the settlers exterminated the few indigenous people who have survived, stripping them of their houses and all their possessions and leaving them nothing for themselves (and these abuses continue to this day). In this regard, their treatment of the locals here has been even worse than on Hispaniola.

They have oppressed the many people of the province, worn them to a shadow and hastened their demise, forcing them to carry over distances of thirty leagues, from the interior of the country to the port, all the blocks of wood and planking needed to make ships and sending them to search for honey and wax up

52 See Introduction, p. xx

in the hills where jaguars tear them to pieces. And they have used and still use even pregnant women and the mothers of newborn babes as beasts of burden.

The most insidious pestilence dreamed up by this governor was the system whereby he granted licences to Spaniards to demand slaves from native caciques and nobles. This development has done more to ravage that country than anything else. Demands for fifty slaves at a time were made every four or five months or whenever an individual obtained permission and a licence from the governor to make such a demand. The demand was always accompanied by the threat that, if the requisite number of slaves was not produced, the noble concerned would be burned alive or thrown to the wild dogs. Since slavery is practically unknown among the local population, even their caciques having at most two or three or four of them, the lords would themselves have to find the slaves. At first they might round up all the orphans they could find; then they might ask any family with two children to surrender one, and a family with three to produce two, thereby fulfilling the demand made of them by the tyrant in their midst. But they did so against a background of wailing and gnashing of teeth, for these people appear to entertain a love for their children which surpasses that of any other people in the world. Since demands of this nature were so frequent, the whole region was devastated within the space of a few years, for during six or seven of the years between 1523 and 1533 five or six slaving vessels patrolled the coast and carted off vast numbers of these innocents to be sold in Panama and Peru, where they all perished. Indeed, experience shows time and time again that these people die very quickly once you remove them from their native lands, especially as they often are forced to go without food while still being made to do a full day's work, those who buy and sell them having no other thought in their heads but the work these slaves can be forced to undertake. In this fashion, more than five hundred thousand poor souls, each of them as free as you or me,[53] have been taken from their homelands. On top of that, a further five or six hundred thousand have so far been killed, either during the course of the hellish fighting initiated by the Spanish or as a direct result of the horrendous conditions in which they have been imprisoned. And the carnage continues to this day. All this devastation has taken place over the past fourteen years, and in the whole of the province of Nicaragua today, once (as I have said) among the most densely populated places on the face of the earth, there remain only four or five thousand people and every day sees even some of these succumb to the work they are made to do, and the personal abuses to which they are subjected every day of their lives.

53 Legally, all Amerindians were subjects of the Crown of Castile and enjoyed equal rights with all other subjects of the Crown. Making war on Amerindians, said the great theologian Francisco de Vitoria, was like making war on the inhabitants of Seville; see Introduction, p. xx, and Pagden, *The Fall of Natural Man*, pp. 29–33

NEW SPAIN

New Spain was discovered in 1517 and, at the time, great
atrocities were committed against the indigenous people of the
region and some were killed by members of the expedition. In
1518 the so-called Christians set about stealing from the people
and murdering them on the pretence of settling the area. And
from that year until this — and it is now 1542 — the great
iniquities and injustices, the outrageous acts of violence and
the bloody tyranny of these Christians have steadily escalated,
the perpetrators having lost all fear of God, all love of their
sovereign, and all sense of self-respect. The heinous outrages
and acts of barbarity have been so vile, the violence so intense,
the murders so frequent, other acts of despotism so extreme,
and the havoc and devastation so widespread throughout the
kingdoms of the Mainland that what we have so far set down
in this account is as nothing compared with what went on in
New Spain, and the scale and nature of the atrocities committed without a break from 1518 right up to this day beggars
description. Even now, in September 1542, the atrocities get
worse by the day, it being the case, as we have said, that the
infernal brutality and utter inhumanity of the acts committed
have steadily increased as time has gone on.

From the very first day they set foot in New Spain, which was
the eighteenth of April 1518, until 1530, there was no respite
whatever in the carnage and mayhem provoked by these cruel
and bloodthirsty Spaniards.[54] Throughout those twelve long

54 Francisco Hernández de Córdoba led the first expedition to Mexico in 1517; he
was followed by Juan de Grijalva in 1518. Both of these, however, were trading
expeditions and neither had formal leave to settle. The first fully equipped
military venture was that led by Cortés which left Cuba on 18 November 1519

years they pillaged their way over an area of some four hundred and fifty leagues around Mexico City, putting those who lived there to the sword and committing all manner of barbarities against them. This area had originally boasted four or five great kingdoms, each of them as large as Spain and a good deal better favoured, and each of them inhabited, as the Almighty had ordained, by more people than the combined population of Toledo, Seville, Valladolid, Saragossa and Barcelona, even when these Spanish cities were at the very height of their fortunes. The whole area veritably teemed with humanity, even though if one were to walk its frontier one would travel over one thousand eight hundred leagues. Yet, over the twelve years of which we are speaking, and during the course of what they term the 'conquest' (which is really and truly nothing other than a series of violent incursions into the territory by these cruel tyrants:[55] incursions condemned not only in the eyes of God but also by law, and in practice far worse than the assaults mounted by the Turk in his attempt to destroy Christendom), the Europeans have, throughout these four hundred and fifty leagues, butchered, burned alive or otherwise done to death four million souls, young and old alike, men, women and children. And this figure does not include those killed and still being killed today as a direct result of the tyrannical slavery and the oppression and privation its victims are forced to endure on a daily basis.

And no account, no matter how lengthy, how long it took to write, nor how conscientiously it was compiled, could possibly do justice to the full horror of the atrocities committed at one time or another in various parts of this region by these mortal enemies of the human race. Even if one were simply to select one or two outrages from among the many, it would still be nigh on impossible to describe them in all their bloody and terrible detail. That said, and even though I am well aware that I can

55 See Introduction, p. xxxix

hardly recount one atrocity in a thousand, I will endeavour to say something about a few of these incidents.

Among other massacres was one which took place in Cholula,[56] a great city of some thirty thousand inhabitants. When all the dignitaries of the city and the region came out to welcome the Spaniards with all due pomp and ceremony, the priests to the fore and the high priest at the head of the procession, and then proceeded to escort them into the city and lodge them in the houses of the lord and the leading citizens, the Spaniards decided that the moment had come to organize a massacre (or 'punishment' as they themselves express such things) in order to inspire fear and terror in all the people of the territory. This was, indeed, the pattern they followed in all the lands they invaded: to stage a bloody massacre of the most public possible kind in order to terrorize those meek and gentle peoples. What they did was the following. They requested the local lord to send for all the nobles and leading citizens of the city and of all the surrounding communities subject to it and, as soon as they arrived and entered the building to begin talks with the Spanish commander, they were seized without anyone outside getting wind of what was afoot. Part of the original request was that they should bring with them five or six thousand native bearers and these were mustered in the courtyards when and as they arrived. One could not watch these poor wretches getting ready to carry the Spaniards' packs without taking pity on them, stark naked as

56 This was Cortés's most spectacular and widely reported massacre. Cholula was a wealthy town on the major Central America trade-route; it was also the cult-centre of Quetzalcoátl, the Mexican deity with whom Cortés is supposed to have been confused. Cortés gave the number of dead as three thousand, but another witness, Vázquez de Tapia, claimed the death toll was ten times higher. The precise figures are irrecoverable; see Cortés, *Letters from Mexico*, pp. 465–6

they were with only their modesty hidden from view, each with a kind of little net on his shoulders in which he carried his own modest store of provisions. They all got down on their haunches and waited patiently like sheep. Once they were all safely inside the courtyard, together with a number of others who were also there at the time, armed guards took up positions covering the exits and Spanish soldiers unsheathed their swords and grasped their lances and proceeded to slaughter these poor innocents. Not a single soul escaped. After a day or two had gone by, several victims surfaced, soaked from head to foot in the blood of their fellows beneath whose bodies they had sheltered (so thick was the carpet of corpses in the courtyard) and, with tears in their eyes, pleaded for their lives; but the Spaniards showed them no mercy nor any compassion, and no sooner did they crawl out from under the pile of corpses than they were butchered. The Spanish commander gave orders that the leading citizens, who numbered over a hundred and were roped together, were to be tied to stakes set in the ground and burned alive. One of these dignitaries, however, who may well have been the first among them and the king of that whole region, managed to get free and took refuge, along with twenty or thirty or forty others, in the great temple of the city, which was fortified and was known in the local language as *quu*.[57] There they put up a stout defence against the Spaniards which lasted for the best part of the day. But the Spaniards, against whom no resistance is really possible, especially when it is mounted by unarmed civilians, set fire to the temple, burning those inside alive, the victims shouting all the time: 'Oh, wicked men! What harm had we done to you? Why do you kill us? Wait till you get to Mexico City, for there our great king, Montezuma,[58] will avenge our deaths.' It is said

57 *Cúe* (or *quu*) was simply the Mexican (Nahuátl) word for a temple
58 There is little substance to this account, as Mexican temples were built of stone and thus could not be destroyed by fire. For the name and title of the Mexican chieftain, normally known in English as Montezuma (from the common Spanish form of his name, Moctezuma), see Cortés, *Letters from Mexico*, p. 460

*The Spanish commander gave orders that the leading citizens
be roped together, tied to stakes and burned alive.*

that, while the Spaniards were slaughtering the five or six
thousand men gathered in the courtyard, their commander regaled his men with snatches of:

> Nero watched from Tarpey's height
> the flames engulf Rome's awesome might;
> children and ancients shout in pain,
> he all regards with cold disdain.[59]

59 A traditional Spanish ballad:

> *Mira Nero de Tarpeya, a Roma cómo se ardía;
> gritos dan niños y viejos, y él de nada se dolía.*

47

They were responsible also for another huge massacre in Tepeaca, a city bigger than Cholula and one with a larger population. Here the Spaniards put countless thousands to the sword in the cruellest possible manner.[60]

From Cholula they made their way to Mexico City.[61] On their journey, they were showered with thousands of gifts from the great king Montezuma who also sent some of his men to stage entertainments and banquets for them on the way. When they reached the Great Causeway which runs for some two leagues right up to the city itself, they were greeted by Montezuma's own brother and many local dignitaries bearing valuable gifts of gold, silver and apparel from the great lord.[62] At the city gates, Montezuma himself came out to meet them, carried on a litter of gold and surrounded by the entire court. He escorted them into the city to the great houses where he had directed they should be lodged. Yet that same day, or so I am reliably informed by a number of eye-witnesses, the Spaniards seized the great king unawares by means of a trick and held him under armed guard of eighty soldiers, eventually putting him in irons.[63] But, leaving aside all of this, although much passed of consequence and one could dwell upon it at length, I should like to relate just one incident contrived by these tyrants. It happened that the Spanish commander had occasion to go to the sea-port to deal with one of his captains who was planning an attack on him,[64] and he left

---

60 For Cortés's account of the attacks mounted against his men in Tepeaca 'from strong and dangerous positions' – which, for reasons he does not explain, led to the attackers' neither 'killing nor wounding a single Spaniard' – see *Letters from Mexico*, pp. 145–8

61 The proper name for the city which Las Casas calls 'Mexico' was Temixtitán or Tenochtitlán

62 Montezuma's brother Cuitlahuac (Cuetravacin) was lord of Yztapalapa, a city through which Cortés had passed on his journey from Cholula. See Cortés's account of this episode in *Letters from Mexico*, pp. 83–4.

63 By Cortés's own account, Montezuma was not seized until more than a week later (*Letters from Mexico*, pp. 88–90)

64 The commander was Cortés, the captain Pánfilo de Narváez. On this expedition and the reasons behind the Narváez expedition, see the essay by J.H. Elliott, 'Cortés, Velázquez, and Charles V', in *Letters from Mexico*, pp. xi–xxxvii (xxiii–xxvi)

*At the city gates, Montezuma himself came out to meet them,
carried on a litter of gold and surrounded by the entire
court.*

another of his henchmen, with a hundred or so men at his
command, to guard King Montezuma while he was away.[65] The
garrison decided to stage a show of strength and thereby boost

[65] The captain left in charge was Pedro de Alvarado, a veteran of Juan de Grijalva's
expedition and effectively second-in-command to Cortés; see J.E. Kelly, *Pedro de
Alvarado, conquistador* (Princeton: Princeton University Press, 1932; reissue Washington, etc.: Kennikat Press, 1971). Cortés's claim that he left Mexico City
garrisoned by 'five hundred men' (*Letters from Mexico*, p. 119) is at odds with eye-
witness accounts which put the number at about one hundred and twenty, many
of them sick and wounded

the fear they inspired in the people of this kingdom, a classic Spanish tactic in these campaigns, as we have had occasion to remark before. All the local citizens, great and small, as well as all the members of the court, were wholly taken up with entertaining their imprisoned lord. To this end, they organized fiestas, some of which involved staging traditional dances every afternoon and evening in squares and residential quarters throughout the city. These dances are called in the local language *mitotes* (those typical of the islands being known as *areitos*);[66] and since these dances are the principal form of public entertainment and enjoyment among the people, they deck themselves out in all their best finery. And the entertainments were organized with close attention to rank and station, the noblest of the citizens dancing nearest the building where their lord was being held. Close by this building, then, danced over two thousand youths of quality, the flower of the nobility of Montezuma's whole empire. Thither the Spanish captain made his way, accompanied by a platoon of his men, under pretence of wanting to watch the spectacle but in fact carrying orders to attack the revellers at a prearranged time, further platoons with identical orders having been despatched to the other squares where entertainments were being staged. The nobles were totally absorbed in what they were doing and had no thought for their own safety when the soldiers drew their swords and shouting: 'For Saint James, and at 'em, men!'[67] proceeded to slice open the lithe and naked bodies of the dancers and to spill their noble blood. Not one dancer was left alive, and the same story was repeated in the other squares throughout the city. This series of events caused horror, anguish and bitterness throughout the land; the whole nation was plunged into mourning and, until the end of time,

66 For a previous reference to *areitos*, see above p. 28
67 Santiago, the name of Saint James of Compostela, was traditionally used by the Spanish as a battle-cry, the legend being that he appeared in person, mounted on a white charger, at the battle of Clavijo against the Moors which supposedly took place in the year 822

or at least as long as a few of these people survive, they will not cease to tell and re-tell, in their *areitos* and dances, just as we do at home in Spain with our ballads, this sad story of a massacre which wiped out their entire nobility, beloved and respected by them for generations and generations.

Once the native population learned of this barbaric and unprecedented outrage, perpetrated against innocent individuals who had done nothing whatever to deserve such cruelty, the whole city, which had up to then tolerated the equally unmerited imprisonment of its lord and master simply because he himself had issued orders that no one was to fight the Christians nor to offer any resistance to them, took up arms and attacked them. Many Spaniards were wounded and only narrowly managed to make good their escape. They ordered Montezuma out on to the terrace at dagger point and forced him to order his men not to attack the house and to cease their insurrection. But the people ceased altogether at that juncture to obey such orders and there was a feeling that they should elect another lord in Montezuma's place who would be able and willing to lead them in battle. At this point, it became known that the Spanish commander was on his way back from the coast after his victory over the rebel forces and that he was not far off and was bringing reinforcements. There followed a lull in the fighting which lasted until he arrived some three or four days later; meanwhile, the number of protesters had swollen with the influx of people from all over the territory. Once the commander arrived, the natives attacked with such unrelenting ferocity that it seemed to the garrison that not one of them would be left alive, and they decided to abandon the city in secret and at night. The locals got wind of this, catching up with many as they fled across the causeways that span the lake and killing them in great numbers,[68] as, indeed, they had every right to, given the attacks we have described that

68 On the site of Tenochtitlán and Cortés's retreat on what became known as the 'Black Night' (*noche triste*), see his *Letters from Mexico*, pp. 131-8

had been made on them: a reasonable and fair-minded man will see that theirs was a defensive action and a just one. The Spaniards then regrouped and there followed a battle for the city in which terrible and bizarre outrages were committed against the indigenous population, vast numbers of whom were killed and many others, several leaders among them, burned alive.[69]

After the vile outrages and abominations perpetrated by the Spaniards, both in Mexico City itself and throughout the whole region (an area of ten or fifteen or twenty leagues all round the city saw countless natives perish at their hands), they transferred their pestilential attentions to the densely populated Pánuco province, where once again they swept through the territory, pillaging and murdering on the grand scale as they went. They then moved on to the provinces of Tuxtepec,[70] Impilcingo,[71] and finally Colima,[72] each one of them greater in extent than the kingdoms of Castile and León, and in each they wrought the same destruction as they had in Mexico City and its province. It would be impracticable to compile a complete dossier of all the atrocities, foul murders and other barbarities they committed, and any such account would be so lengthy it would prove impossible for the reader to take in.

It should be recalled that the pretext upon which the Spanish invaded each of these provinces and proceeded to massacre the people and destroy their lands – lands which teemed with people and should surely have been a joy and a delight to any true Christian – was purely and simply that they were making good the claim of the Spanish Crown to the territories in question. At no stage had any order been issued entitling them to massacre the people or to enslave them. Yet, whenever the natives did not drop everything and rush to recognize publicly the truth of the

69 Las Casas is here conflating two events: the retreat which took place in 1520 and the siege of the city by Cortés the following year
70 Variously 'Tatutepeque', 'Tuchitebeque', 'Tututepec', or 'Tuxtepeque'
71 Or 'Ipilcingo'
72 Also known as 'Colimán' or 'Alimán'

irrational and illogical claims that were made, and whenever they did not immediately place themselves completely at the mercy of the iniquitous and cruel and bestial individuals who were making such claims, they were dubbed outlaws and held to be in rebellion against His Majesty. This, indeed, was the tenor of the letters that were sent back to the Spanish court, and everybody involved in the administration of the New World was blind to the simple truth enshrined in the first principles of law and government that nobody who is not a subject of a civil power in the first place can be deemed in law to be in rebellion against that power. Any reasonable person who knows anything of God, of rights and of civil law can imagine for himself what the likely reaction would be of any people living peaceably within their own frontiers, unaware that they owe allegiance to anyone save their natural lords, were a stranger suddenly to issue a demand along the following lines: 'You shall henceforth obey a foreign king, whom you have never seen nor ever heard of and, if you do not, we will cut you to pieces' – especially when they discover that these strangers are indeed quite prepared to carry out this threat to the letter. Even more shocking is the fact that when the local people do obey such commands they are harshly treated as common slaves, put to hard labour and subjected to all manner of abuse and to agonizing torments that ensure a slower and more painful death than would summary execution. Indeed, for them, the end result is the same: they, their wives and their children all perish and the whole of their nation is wiped from the face of the earth. And so blinded by ambition and driven by greed are the devils who advocate such treatment of these people that they cannot see that, when their victims come to obey under duress this foreign overlord and publicly recognize his authority over them, simply because of their fear of what will happen to them if they do not, such a recognition of suzerainty has no standing in law whatever, any such prerogative obtained by menaces from any people anywhere in the world being invalid. In practice, the only rights these perfidious crusaders have earned which can be upheld in human, divine, or natural law are the right to eternal damnation and the right to answer for the offences and the harm they have done the Spanish Crown by utterly ruining every one of these kingdoms and (as far as it is within their power) invalidating all claims the Spanish Crown may have to the territories of the New World. These, then, are the true services they have performed and continue to perform for their sovereign in this part of the world.

With this same unimpeachable title to possession, this tyrant of a commander sent two of his captains, both of them even more ferocious and barbaric, more implacable and merciless than he was himself, to two vast, prosperous and highly favoured kingdoms, sharing a common frontier and some three hundred leagues from Mexico City. The first of these two densely populated realms, Guatemala, lies on the Pacific; the other, known as Naco and Honduras (or Guaimura), has an Atlantic seaboard.[73] Both expeditionary forces were well-manned, with both cavalry and infantry, the commander sending one overland and the other by sea.[74]

It is no exaggeration to say that one could make a whole book – and a book that would stagger not only contemporaries but future generations also – out of the atrocities, barbarities, murders, clearances, ravages and other foul injustices perpetrated by members of these two expeditions, and particularly by those that went to Guatemala, the leader of the other expedition coming to an abrupt and sticky end.[75] Here were abominations that not

73 Las Casas calls the Pacific 'the southern shore' and the Atlantic 'the northern shore' (e.g. below, p. 63)
74 The overland expedition to Guatemala was under the command of Pedro de Alvarado (see above, p. 49, n. 65), the fleet headed for Honduras under that of Cristóbal de Olid. Alvarado's own account of the conquest of Guatemala is contained in his two surviving letters to Cortés, reproduced in English translation in Patricia de Fuentes, *The Conquistadores* (New York: Orion Press, 1963), pp. 182–96, and used extensively by Las Casas in compiling the present account
75 For an account of Olid's drumhead court-marshal and execution at the hands of Francisco de Las Casas and Gil González Dávila, see Cortés, *Letters from Mexico*, p. 412 and Robert S. Chamberlain, *The Conquest and Colonization of Honduras, 1502–1550* (Washington D.C.: Carnegie Institute, 1953), pp. 11–14

only outdid, in number and in kind, everything that had been seen before in the New World but also went far beyond those perpetrated by contemporaries, vast tracts of land being laid waste and turned into desert and an incalculable number of natives killed.

The seaborne expedition sacked the towns all along the coast, committing all manner of violence against the people who lived there, as, for example, when the locals of Yucatán, a province which lay on their route to the kingdom of Naco and Guaimura, whither the Spaniards were headed, came out to greet them and offer them gifts and then the Spaniards, once they had landed, sent out raiding parties throughout the territory, robbing and killing and destroying everything and everyone in sight. There was one Spanish captain who mutinied and, taking three hundred men with him, set off inland towards the kingdom of Guatemala, burning and looting the towns, and robbing and killing those who lived there. He deliberately followed such a scorched-earth policy for some one hundred and twenty leagues, so that, should his erstwhile companions-in-arms decide on pursuit, they would find the whole region empty and barren, and all the local people athirst to take revenge on their pursuers in return for the harm and destruction wrought by him and his men. A few days later the officer in overall charge of the expedition, against whom he had mutinied, was killed and his place taken by a whole series of barbaric despots who inflicted unspeakable cruelty on the natives, butchering them, enslaving them and selling them to merchant-sailors in exchange for wine, clothing and other things. The despotism of the invaders and the enslavement of the population led, between 1524 and 1535, to the complete destruction of all the territories of the kingdom of Naco and Honduras, once a veritable paradise on earth supporting a denser population than anywhere else in the world. Nowadays, when one travels through this area, one sees nothing but bare, ruined settlements, and the whole melancholy spectacle is enough to melt the hardest of hearts.[76] During these eleven years, more than two million souls have perished and, in an area of more than a hundred leagues by a hundred leagues, only two thousand survivors are to be seen; and even this number is shrinking day by day as the survivors succumb to the rigours of a life of slavery.

Turning our attention once more to the implacable tyrant in charge of the Guatemala expedition, we find him outdoing, as we have already had occasion to remark, all his predecessors in cruelty and barbarism, rivalling in wickedness even those who are active in the area today. He covered (as he was to report back to the commander who had sent the expedition) a distance of some four hundred leagues, from the provinces around Mexico City to the Guatemala border, killing and stealing, burning and pillaging. His pretext for destroying everything and everyone in his path was the one we have seen invoked before: that the locals must recognize the suzerainty of a bunch of inhuman and unjust barbarians who proclaimed themselves the representatives of a Spanish sovereign the locals had never seen, of whom they had never heard, and whom they soon judged to be even more cruel than his agents, for he and his men never allowed the people time to think over the implications of this proclamation, but fell upon them, killing and burning, the minute it had been read.

76 Las Casas is presumably alluding to his journey through the area in 1540 on his way to take ship for Europe

THE PROVINCE AND KINGDOM OF GUATEMALA

As soon as he set foot in the kingdom of Guatemala, this tyrant proceeded to kill the inhabitants in large numbers. None the less, the chief of Utatlán, the largest city in the kingdom,[77] came out to receive him with all due ceremony, having himself carried out of the city on a litter amid fanfares of trumpets and the beating of war-drums, staging lavish entertainments to mark his arrival, setting before the visitors a sumptuous banquet, and inviting them to make free with whatever they could provide. That night, the Spaniards camped outside the city, impressed as they were by the defences and afraid that they might be in danger if they risked spending the night within the walls. On the morrow, the Spanish captain summoned the chief and the leading citizens and when they came, all unsuspecting, he seized them and demanded a certain sum of gold. When they replied that they had none, there being no gold in Guatemala, he declared them guilty on that count alone and without any due process of law directed that they be burned alive. Once the lords of the other provinces of the kingdom learned that he had burned their chief and his nobles simply because they had refused him gold, they fled their towns and cities and took to the mountains, leaving instructions to their people that they should go and offer to serve the Spaniards but not disclose where it was that the lords had gone into hiding. When the local people duly approached the Spaniards, declaring themselves willing to recognize them as their masters and to serve them in whatever

---

77 Utatlán (or Uclalán), known to its original inhabitants as Gumarkaaj and capital of the Quiché kingdom, stood near the modern town of Santa Cruz de Quiché. The chief mentioned here was Tecum Uman, later assassinated by Alvarado

capacity they should choose, this most Christian of commanders replied that he was not prepared to have them enter his service but would kill every single one of them unless they revealed the whereabouts of their chiefs. Their response to this was that, as they knew nothing of where their chiefs had gone, the Spaniards would do better to take them into their service and that they would be at home, awaiting their pleasure. There, as they several times insisted, the Spaniards could kill them or do what they would with them, their women and their children. The extraordinary thing is that the Spaniards then did go to the towns and villages where they found these poor people, in the shelter of their own homes, living and working peacefully with their families and that, catching them unawares, they did then proceed to cut them to pieces one and all. One very large and important city, where the inhabitants were more than usually incautious and innocently believed themselves to be quite safe, was almost entirely destroyed by the Spanish within the space of two hours, and all the inhabitants who did not manage to flee were put to the sword: women, children and old men.

Once the natives saw that their deep humility, generosity and submissiveness did nothing to soften the hearts of these ravening beasts, and that the Spaniards were prepared to hack them to pieces for absolutely no reason whatever, they decided that, although they stood no chance of defeating ferocious enemies who were on horseback and were armed to the teeth, they might as well die as men in defence of their homes, standing shoulder to shoulder and, insofar as they could, avenging themselves on their wicked and hellish enemies, even though they were well aware that, weak as they were, on foot and unarmed, they were doomed to die whatever they did. They hit upon the notion of digging holes in the middle of the roads so that any horse being ridden along that stretch of road would fall into the hole and impale itself on the deadly staves which they sharpened and blackened by fire before setting them into the floor of the pit. They covered the pits with turf and other grasses so that there

All those captured – pregnant women, mothers of newborn babes, children and old men – were thrown into the pits and impaled alive.

should be no sign of anything out of the ordinary. Once or twice a horse did fall into these pits but only rarely as the Spaniards soon learned to keep an eye open for them. But, in order to avenge themselves on the local people for having devised this trick, they decreed that all natives taken alive, of any station and of all ages, should themselves be cast into the pits they had dug, and so it came to pass that all those they captured – pregnant women, mothers of newborn babes, children and old men – were thrown into these pits and impaled on the spikes. The pits, brim-full of their wretched victims, afforded a sorry spectacle, especially as they included women with their children still clutched to their breasts. Those they did not deal with in this fashion, they transfixed on their lances or stabbed to death with their daggers, or threw to the wild dogs who tore them to pieces and ate them. On the odd occasion when they found a native of rank among their haul, they did him the honour of burning him alive. This inhumane butchery continued unabated for a full seven years, from 1524 until 1530 or 1531, and the reader can imagine for himself the sheer numbers involved.

Among the countless atrocities committed by this butcher and his brothers (who were every bit as ruthless as him, as indeed were all the other commanders in his company), one stands out as being worthy of record.[78] In the city of Cuzcatlán,[79] very near where the town of San Salvador stands today and at that time the capital of a rich province running along the Pacific coast for some forty or fifty leagues and also called Cuzcatlán, the local people mounted a huge formal welcome for this butcher, with some twenty or thirty thousand of them lining the streets to offer hens and other foodstuffs. No sooner had he received these gifts than he instructed every man in his entourage to take as many of the locals as he wanted to act as his servants during his stay in the area and to minister to his needs. Most of them took at least fifty, some as many as a hundred, depending on how many each judged he would need to satisfy his every whim. These poor wretches went unprotestingly, like lambs to the slaughter, to the man who selected them, doing everything their new master asked of them and treating him almost as a god. The Spanish captain, meanwhile, requested the local dignitaries to bring him large quantities of gold, this being the main object of the expedition. The locals said that they would willingly give him all the gold they had and collected together a vast number

78 Pedro de Alvarado took three of his brothers on the Guatemala expedition: Gonzalo, Gómez and Jorge; see Kelly, *Pedro de Alvarado*, pp. 121–55
79 Las Casas gives this as 'Cuzcatán'

of the gilt copper hatchets that are in common use among them and which have the appearance of gold because they do have some gold in them. The captain ordered his men to test them by scratching the surface of the metal and, as soon as he saw that they were in fact made of copper, addressed his men, saying: 'The Devil take this place. There is no gold for us here, men. Let's be off, and let each take with him his local servants, put them in chains and brand them as slaves.' And this is what they did, tying up everyone they could catch and branding them, and I myself saw the son of one of the leading citizens of the city branded with His Majesty's mark as a common slave. Once the people of the area and those from the town who had managed to escape the clutches of the Spaniards saw the evil that was being wrought upon their fellow-countrymen, they began to band together and take up arms against their tormentors. In the ensuing fighting, the Spaniards inflicted heavy losses upon them and committed all kinds of atrocities before returning to Guatemala and building the city that has only recently been visited by the full force of Divine Justice and been utterly destroyed by three violent disasters, the first lashing it with heavy rain, the second burying it beneath a deluge of earth, and the third pulverizing it with hailstones the size of ten or twenty oxen.[80] Thus it was that, in this way and in others, they plundered and ravaged an area of more than a hundred leagues by a hundred leagues that was among the most fertile and most heavily peopled on earth, killing all the leaders among the native population and, with all men of military age dead, reducing the survivors to the Hell of slavery. And when they pressed for further slaves to be handed over by way of tribute, the natives gave up their own sons and daughters, as they had no further slaves to surrender, and all were sent by boat to Peru to be auctioned. As this very butcher himself was quite accurately to record in writing, there were more people in this region than in the whole of the

80 Possibly Antigua, which was hit by a hurricane in September 1541

The blackguard set the royal seal of approval on the establishment, in his camp, of a human abattoir.

kingdom of Mexico. Yet, in this same area, he and his brothers, together with their comrades-in-arms, were responsible for the deaths of more than four or five million souls over the fifteen or sixteen years, from 1524 to 1540, that they were in the area. Nor is the butchery and destruction over, for those natives who have survived so far will soon perish in the same ways as have all the others in the region.

One of this blackguard's ploys, whenever he was about to attack a city or the surrounding countryside, was to take with him as many natives as he could from the tribes he had already conquered and to get them to do his fighting for him. Since he never fed the ten or twenty thousand impressed natives in his army, he gave them leave to eat the prisoners they took, thus setting the royal seal of approval on the establishment, in his camp, of a human abattoir where he himself would preside over the slaughter and grilling of children and where grown men were butchered for the sake of their hands and feet which were generally held to be the best cuts. As news spread of these atrocities, all the other peoples of the region were paralysed with fear, as were those elsewhere in the country.

Another occupation in which the natives perished wholesale was shipbuilding. For a distance of one hundred and thirty leagues, from the Atlantic to the Pacific, he had natives carry anchors weighing three and four *quintales*.[81] So heavy were these that the flukes of the anchor would bite deep into their bare shoulders and backs. He used these same naked and defenceless people to transport cannon overland,[82] and I myself saw many of them stumbling along in agony. He broke up families, dishonouring the native men by taking their wives and daughters and keeping the good will of his fighting men and his mariners by letting them carry off the women on board their vessels. He loaded his boats to the gunwales with natives, and his greed was such that all on board perished of hunger and thirst. And, if one were to set out in detail all the atrocities he committed, they would make a very weighty tome indeed, and one which would truly shock the world. He mounted two expeditions by sea, each consisting of many vessels, and with these he scorched the whole region as though he were the avenging fire sent from Heaven.[83] Oh, if one were to catalogue all those orphaned by him, all those whose children he stole, all those whose wives he took, all the women he widowed, and all the adultery, violence and rape that

81 The imperial Spanish *quintal* weighed one hundred pounds
82 Las Casas here uses the term 'cannon' to invoke an image of the artillery trains of European armies. Alvarado would have had only a few mortars
83 The first expedition was to Peru in 1534; the second, which was to have sailed under Alvarado to the Spice Islands in 1541, never got off the ground

could be laid at his door, as well as all those he deprived of liberty, and all the torment and calamity countless people suffered because of him! If one could calculate how many tears were shed and how many sighs and anguished groans were caused by his actions, how much grief he occasioned in this life, and how many souls he consigned to eternal damnation in the life hereafter – not only the countless hordes of natives, but also the Christian wretches whose association with him led them to commit vile atrocities, mortal sins and inhuman barbarity. May God have mercy on him and may He be satisfied with the terrible death which He visited on him.[84]

84 Alvarado was killed in a skirmish in Nochistlán in July 1541

In 1525, in the wake of the barbarity and carnage we have described and of yet further atrocities committed in the provinces of New Spain and Pánuco, there arrived yet another butcher who was to be responsible for outrage upon outrage in Pánuco province.[85] He it was who saw to the depopulation of the entire province, for he took to branding any number of free men as slaves, in the same way as we have seen others do before him, and bundling them on to vessel after vessel for transport to the island slave-markets of Cuba and Hispaniola where they would fetch a better price. He also bartered one mare against eighty locals: against, that is, eighty members of the human race. He was later appointed as governor of Mexico City and of the whole of New Spain, presiding over the *Audiencia*[86] there with a number of fellow-villains as his magistrates. Together, they conspired to effect a devastation that beggars all description, committing outrages and atrocities, robberies and every other form of abomination. They brought the whole province to such a state that, had God not cut short their efforts, first through the opposition mounted by Franciscan friars and then through the establishment of a godly and just *Audiencia*, they would, within

85 Beltrán Nuño de Guzmán. For an account of Nuño in English, characterizing him as 'a natural gangster', see J.H. Parry, *The Audiencia of New Galicia in the Sixteenth Century* (Cambridge: Cambridge University Press, 1948; reprinted 1968), pp. 19–26
86 The *Audiencias*, or Chanceries, were royal courts of justice, normally presided over by a high-ranking churchman but staffed by qualified lawyers. The first such body was established in Castile in the mid-fifteenth century. In the New World, the *Audiencias* had far greater authority than in mainland Spain and were intimately involved in the government of the colony in question. The magistrates (*oidores*) in this first *Audiencia* of New Spain, presided over by Nuño de Guzmán, were Paredes, Francisco Maldonado, Matienzo and Delgadillo

the space of two short years, have reduced the whole of New Spain to that state of utter wretchedness that now greets the visitor to the island of Hispaniola.[87] For example, one of this man's companions-in-arms decided that he would have a wall built to enclose some land he had acquired, imported eight thousand natives to work, unpaid and unfed, on this project, and took not a blind bit of notice when one after another they dropped dead of hunger.

Once he learned that a new *Audiencia* had been appointed and was already on its way, this villain, already responsible for bringing Pánuco province to its knees, set off inland in search of fresh fields for his talents, taking with him some fifteen or twenty thousand hapless Mexicans to carry his baggage and that of his fellow-Spaniards; of the native bearers, fewer than two hundred were to survive the journey, all the others perishing *en route*. When he fetched up in the province of Michoacán, some forty leagues from Mexico City and yet another area every bit as fertile and populous as Mexico itself, the lord of Michoacán came out in solemn procession with many of his people to welcome him and his men and offer them every kindness, showering them all the while with gifts.[88] This lord had the reputation of being extremely wealthy and of having much gold and silver in his possession, and so the Spaniards seized him and, in an attempt to force him to hand over his treasures, proceeded to torture him in the fashion I shall now describe. They put him in fetters and tied his hands to a plank which ran the full length of his body; they then lit a brazier under the soles of his feet and had a lad with a hyssop filled with oil sprinkle them from time

---

87 The first Franciscans, known as 'the Twelve', arrived in 1524. The *oidores* of the second *Audiencia*, convened under the presidency of Francisco Ramírez de Fuenleal, bishop of Santo Domingo, were Vasco de Quiroga (the first bishop of Michoacán), Alonso Maldonado, Juan de Salmerón and Francisco de Ceynos; see Arthur S. Aiton, *Antonio de Mendoza, First Viceroy of New Spain* (Durham North Carolina: Duke University Press, 1927), p. 58

88 The lord of the independent Tarascan state of Michoacán was known as the *cazonci*, or *catzontzin*

to time to ensure a nice even roasting. On one side of the hapless victim stood one tormentor holding an armed crossbow pointed at his heart, while on the other stood a second holding a wild dog which constantly snapped at him and which would have torn him to pieces in the twinkling of an eye. They went on torturing him in this way, trying to get him to reveal the whereabouts of the gold and silver he was supposed to possess, until a Franciscan finally got wind of what was going on and came and released him, although the poor man later died of the injuries they had inflicted. This is only one instance of the treatment meted out to the lords and leading citizens of these provinces; many others were tortured and murdered in similar fashion, in the hope that they could be made to hand over gold and silver.

Another of these bullies was appointed at this time as Inspector of Indian Affairs,[89] although, in the event, he was to prove less interested in their physical and spiritual welfare than he was in their purses and their lands. When he discovered that a number of them still had idols hidden away, the wretched Spaniards never having taken the trouble to teach them a word about another and better God, he seized them and tortured them into surrendering these idols, thinking they would be made of gold and silver. When he discovered that they were not, he was so determined not to lose out on a single opportunity to make money, which was what he was after, that he forced his victims to bring him all the gold and silver they could lay their hands on so that they might buy back their gods and worship them in the traditional manner. This is yet another example of the great deeds of these benighted Spaniards and of the ways in which they bring lustre and honour to the name of the Lord.

This same butcher then journeyed from Michoacán to the province of Jalisco, which was at that time still virgin territory to the Spanish. One of the most fertile and wonderful parts of the New World, it was home to a huge number of people who

89 The Spanish term is *visitador*, literally, 'visitor'

lived there undisturbed in harmony and comfort. One of the principal settlements was itself as much as seven leagues broad. When the Spaniards arrived, the local people came out to welcome them with smiling faces and bearing gifts, as is the custom throughout the New World. But this wretch immediately embarked upon the by now habitual Spanish policy of inflicting pain and terror upon them, acknowledging no limits to his frenzied quest for his great God, gold. He burned towns and cities to the ground, seized the local lords, torturing them and enslaving all those he could lay his hands upon. He led away thousands in chains, burdening women who had recently given birth with his baggage and that of his wicked companions so that, what with the huge loads they had to carry and the hunger they were forced to endure, they could no longer carry their children as well and were forced to leave them by the side of the road where they perished in huge numbers.

One Spaniard, who wished to satisfy his evil lust on a young girl, took out his dagger – or as it may be his sword – and cut off the hand of the girl's mother who was trying to wrench her from his grasp. When the girl persisted in refusing him, he stabbed her to death.

Although these people had afforded him every welcome as an honoured guest, this commander caused four thousand five hundred of them to be branded as common slaves, even though, legally, they were all free, as, indeed, are all the indigenous peoples of the New World. Nor did he make any difference between men and women, taking and branding even the children from one to five years of age, some of them still unweaned. And he committed other atrocities too many and too dreadful to recount.

After numerous iniquitous attacks on the native population during the course of which, and quite without provocation, he was responsible for carnage on a grand scale, he proceeded to impose throughout the area the reign of terror so beloved of Spanish butchers in the New World, allowing free rein to the officers under his command to inflict unprecedented barbarities upon the local people in order to squeeze gold and other offerings out of them. One of his officers was responsible for the indiscriminate slaughter of many locals, hanging some, burning others alive, and throwing yet others to wild dogs, sometimes sawing off their hands and feet, sometimes pulling out their tongues or hacking off their heads. Even though the locals never raised a finger against the Spaniards, the distinguished commander knowingly allowed this spate of atrocities to continue unchecked, directed as it was to terrorizing the local people into doing his bidding and into bringing him gifts of gold or other precious objects. On top of this, the Spaniards inflicted pain and untold misery on the entire native population, subjecting them to an unrelenting daily – even hourly – round of lashes, beatings, and cruel treatment of every kind.

It is said that this man was directly responsible for the looting and destruction of eight hundred towns and villages throughout the kingdom of Jalisco and that it was because of his harsh treatment that the local people, seeing all around them perish under the Spanish yoke, were driven to despair and, fleeing into the mountains, finally began to offer a measure of organized resistance, killing a handful of their oppressors, as in all justice they were fully entitled to do. As they were subjected to more and yet more injustice by Spaniards passing through the region on their way to tyrannize other provinces (or, as they would put it, 'explore' them), many fortified themselves in certain mountain redoubts, although even there they were prey to the ferocious assaults which have ravaged and all but depopulated the entire province and which have occasioned the deaths of countless innocents. The wretched Spaniards, having abandoned all Christian sense of right and wrong and been totally given over to a reprobate mind,[90] are utterly impervious both to the justice of the actions of the local inhabitants and to the rights these people

90 See above, p. 3, note 1

quite properly enjoy under natural, divine, and Roman law to defend themselves by cutting the Spanish forces to pieces and, if only they were sufficient in number and possessed of the necessary weapons, throwing them out of their land once and for all. The Spanish also prove blind to their own wickedness in persisting in waging war (even though such a course of action is condemned by all the laws known to man) on a people on whom they have previously inflicted unpardonable wrongs and towards whom they have behaved in an evil and wicked fashion. On the contrary, they now proclaim and record for posterity their conviction that the 'victories' they continue to enjoy over an innocent local population, by dint of massacring them, come from God, and that their wicked campaigns in the New World amount to a just war; and they take care to give paeans of praise to the Lord and to recognize the part He has played in their success and His gift to them of wickedness, just like the thieves of whom the prophet Zechariah says, in Chapter 11: 'Thus saith the Lord my God; Feed the flock of the slaughter; Whose possessors slay them, and hold themselves not guilty; and they that sell them say, Blessed be the Lord; for I am rich.'[91]

91 Zechariah 11: 4–5

THE KINGDOM OF YUCATÁN

The year 1526 saw yet another thorough scoundrel elevated to a position of power, this time as governor of the kingdom of Yucatán.[92] As others seeking office in the New World had done before him, this man made false claims at court and made promises he had no intention of keeping in order to secure for himself a position and an authority which he then proceeded to use to feather his own nest at the expense of those he was appointed to govern. The kingdom of Yucatán was very densely populated, for it enjoys a healthy climate and produces foodstuffs in plenty, even more so than Mexico province. This kingdom, some three hundred leagues in perimeter, is particularly well endowed with fruit of all kinds, and produces more honey and wax than has been discovered to date in any other part of the New World. The inhabitants stood out from all their neighbours not only on account of their virtue and their level of civilization but also because they were freer than any of their neighbours from the taint of sin and vice. Among all the peoples of the region they seemed the fittest to hear the word of God, and their territory the best suited by Nature to the establishment of towns and cities, where the local people might have lived side by side in peace and prosperity with the Spanish, who would then have found themselves, had they only proved worthy, in a paradise on earth. But the Spaniards were utterly unfit for such a future, their savage greed and manifest sinfulness rendering them as unworthy of such a paradise here as they had in every other

92 Francisco de Montejo (?1479–1553), who had been one of Cortés's companions in 1519 and conquered much of the Yucatán Peninsula between 1526 and 1537. His son, also named Francisco, founded the city of Mérida there in 1542

region of the New World the Almighty had consented that the Spanish should discover. The poor innocent people of the area, who simply stayed in their homes and gave not the slightest indication of ill will towards the Spanish, found themselves attacked in the most vicious manner by this butcher and the three hundred men under his command, and many were killed. If there had been any gold in this province, the Spaniards would have finished off the local population by sending them down mines to dig it out of the earth; as it was, the only way they could realize a profit from the bodies and souls of these poor wretches for whom our Lord died on the Cross was to enslave all those whom they had not already murdered, and this they proceeded to do indiscriminately, bartering with the masters of the vessels that came in number to the region once it became known that slaves were to be had in exchange for goods. Natives were sold to buy wine, oil, and vinegar, salt pork, items of clothing, a horse, or whatever else the butcher and his men imagined they might need. A man would be invited to choose from among fifty or a hundred young girls the one he most fancied, and she would then be handed over in exchange for an *arroba*[93] of wine or oil or vinegar, or for a side of salt pork. Two or three hundred young men would be lined up in similar fashion, the price being much the same. It happened that one young man, the son of a chief, was traded for a cheese; on another occasion a hundred natives were exchanged for a single horse. This went on for seven years, from 1526 until 1533, and during that time the whole region was devastated and the native population enslaved or massacred without quarter. In 1533, the people of the area were granted a short respite from this Hell, with the Spaniards leaving in response to news that great wealth was to be had in Peru; but it was not long before the commanders were back and the hellish round of atrocities, robberies and enslavement was once again in full swing. It still goes on today, and the

93 See above, p. 24, note 32

One woman, determined that the dogs should not tear her to pieces, tied her child to her leg, and hanged herself from a beam.

whole region of three hundred leagues, once, as we have said, so full of bustle and life, is now almost entirely abandoned.

There is no way the written word can convey the full horror of the atrocities committed throughout this region; nor, even if it were to, would the reader credit the excesses that such an account would reveal. I shall accordingly give details of but two or three incidents. The wretched Spaniards actively pursued the locals, both men and women alike, using wild dogs to track them and hunt them down. One woman, who was indisposed at the time and so not able to make good her escape, determined that the dogs should not tear her to pieces as they had done her neighbours and, taking a rope, and tying her one-year-old child to her leg, hanged herself from a beam. Yet she was not in time to prevent the dogs from ripping the infant to pieces, even though a friar did arrive and baptize the infant before it died.

When the Spaniards were in the very act of leaving the province, one of them demanded that the son of a local chief go with him, but the boy declined, adamant that he did not want to leave home. The Spaniard retorted: 'You will come with me or I will cut off both your ears.' When the boy persisted, repeating that he had no wish to leave home, the Spaniard took out his dagger and lopped off first one of his ears and then the other. When the boy again insisted that he did not want to go with him, he hacked off his nose, laughing out loud as he did so as though he were doing no more than pull his hair playfully.

This was the same fiend who was later to boast to a venerable cleric, without any sign of shame or remorse, that he always laboured long and hard to make the local women pregnant so that they would fetch a higher price as slaves.

It was in this kingdom, or in one of the provinces of New Spain, that a Spaniard who was out hunting deer or rabbits realized that his dogs were hungry and, not finding anything they could hunt, took a little boy from his mother, cut his arms and legs into chunks with his knife and distributed them among his dogs. Once they had eaten up these steaks, he threw the rest of the carcass on the ground for them to fight over. These examples should suffice to give some idea of the brutality of the Spanish throughout this territory, of how far God has given them over to a reprobate mind,[94] and of the attitude they take towards a local people created in God's image and redeemed by His blood. Yet, as we shall see, worse was to come.

Without dwelling on atrocities too many and too horrible to

94 See above, p. 3, note 1

imagine committed throughout this kingdom by those calling themselves Christians, I should like to close my account with the following incident. As soon as these hellhounds had left, dazzled as they were by the prospect of the riches of Peru, Brother Jacob and four fellow-members of the Order of Saint Francis determined to go to the area to calm the native population, preach to them and bring to the love of Christ those who had survived the Hell that was seven years of continual Spanish tyranny.[95] They set off, I believe, in 1534, sending on ahead of them a number of natives of the province of Mexico to act as messengers and to ask whether the people would permit the brothers to come among them and to preach their gospel of a single God, the true Lord of Creation. The locals took advice and debated long and hard among themselves, asking what kind of men these were who called themselves 'Father' and 'Brother', what was it they were after, and in what ways were they different from the 'Christians' who had committed such injustices against them and done them such grievous harm. They finally agreed to let them come among them, provided they came alone and brought no Spaniards with them. The friars undertook to respect these conditions, which had in any case the prior approval of the Viceroy of New Spain,[96] agreeing that only friars would enter the lands in question, that no Spaniard would accompany them, and that there would be no repetition of the atrocities that had been committed by Christians in the recent past. They preached Christ's Gospel in the usual way and also taught the people about the good and godly intentions of the King of Spain towards them. The local people were so affected by the doctrine and good example of the friars and so delighted by what they told them of the kings of Spain (for throughout the previous seven years no one had ever breathed a word in their hearing about there being any king save the governor who mistreated

95 Jacobo de Tastera (or Testera), O.S.F., was a personal friend of Las Casas
96 Antonio de Mendoza, who did not in fact arrive in Mexico until late 1535

and slaughtered them) that the mission was only forty days old when the local chiefs brought all the idols they had previously worshipped and handed them over to the missionaries for burning as well as entrusting them with the schooling of their children who are the apples of their eyes. They built churches and temples and houses for the friars while invitations poured in from other areas of the country from local people who wished to hear the word of God and to learn more about this great King of Castile. They also did something previously unheard of in the New World (reports of similar happenings written by those who had tyrannized the local people and destroyed vast swathes of their land in the New World being nothing but a pack of lies): at the suggestion of the brothers, twelve or fifteen local lords, each with dominion over many subjects and each the owner of large estates, gathered together their people and, with their full approval, voluntarily subjected themselves and them to the Spanish Crown, acknowledging the Emperor as their supreme lord in his capacity as King of Spain, and appending their marks (as they could not write their names) to a number of documents which I have in my possession together with the sworn testimony of the missionaries themselves.

It was at this point, with these people well on the road to the love of Christ and the friars joyful in the belief that they would be able to convert all the people of the kingdom (or at least the not inconsiderable number who had survived the slaughter and barbarity of the past several years), that a band of thirty Spaniards irrupted on to the scene, eighteen of them on horseback and a further twelve on foot. These brigands brought with them bundles of idols they had looted from the people in other parts of the country and their leader instructed one of the local lords to take the idols and distribute them throughout the territory. The price for each was set at one slave, male or female; and the chief was warned that, unless he complied, the Spaniards would attack his people. This threat was enough to frighten the chief into doing what they wanted and he duly distributed the idols throughout his lands, instructing his subjects to worship them and to surrender men and women as Spanish slaves. The people were cowed into compliance with this sacrilegious traffic, those families with two children handing over one and those with three two, and the local chief in this way satisfied the greed of Spaniards whom I cannot bring myself to dignify with the name of Christians.

One of these blasphemous and ungodly bandits, a certain Juan García,[97] being ill and on the point of death, instructed his Amerindian slave-girl that the two sackfuls of idols he kept under his bed should under no circumstances be bartered but that, since they were of good quality, she should insist on getting the proper price of one slave for each. With this thought on his mind and these words on his lips he died. Who can doubt but that this wretch is now plunged into the depths of Hell?

We are now in a position to reflect on just how these Spaniards have improved the life of the peoples of the New World, alerting them to the true Faith, teaching by example and bringing honour to the name of the Lord. We have seen them strive to ensure that He is known to these people and worshipped by them; we have witnessed Spanish concern that the true Faith should take root, grow and blossom among them; and we can judge whether the sins of the Spanish are any less grave than that of Jeroboam who made Israel to sin when he struck the two golden calves for gods, or whether they are any less grave than that of Judas Iscariot, or their consequences any the less terrible; for time and again the Spaniard in the New World, overcome by his lust for gold, has betrayed the Lord, and time and again he has denied Him, the betrayals and the denials continuing down to the present day.

Once the local people saw that the undertaking given by the

97 This is one of the very few occasions in the *Short Account* on which Las Casas names one of the 'blackguards' he is attacking. However, the name is too common for any identification to be possible

missionaries that they would ensure that Spaniards would be excluded from the territory had not been honoured, and that it was those selfsame Spaniards who now brought idols and made them buy them after they had surrendered all their own gods to the friars for burning in return for the promise of one single God they could worship, they were beside themselves and, as one man, rose in revolt against the missionaries, asking them: 'Why did you lie to us? Why did you trick us with your promise that you would keep the Spanish out of our territory? Why did you burn our gods when you knew they would bring us others from other parts of the country which we would have to buy? Were not our own gods better than those of other people?' The brother friars did the best they could to appease them, but had no real answer to their questions. They did seek out the band of thirty and explained to them the harm they had done, pleading with them to be gone, but the Spaniards refused and even gave the locals to understand that they had come at the express invitation of the missionaries, which was a barefaced lie. The people eventually determined to kill the friars and they only managed to escape by night after they had been warned of the plan by one or two locals. It was only after they had left that the people realized that they had been innocent all along and that it was the Spaniards who had lied. They sent messengers over fifty leagues to plead with them to return, begging them to forgive the hostility shown towards them. Being true servants of God and having the souls of the people at heart, the missionaries agreed; when they returned, they found themselves welcomed as angels and remained in the area four or five months, during all of which time the local people showered kindnesses on them. Eventually, however, given that the soldiers showed no signs of leaving, that (because Yucatán is so far from New Spain) the Viceroy proved unable to shift them even by having them publicly declared traitors, and that they continued to maltreat and abuse the local population in their usual manner, it seemed to the missionaries that, sooner or later, the people would be provoked beyond measure and might even see the friars as scapegoats, especially as it was proving impossible to preach calmly to a local population that was, like the friars themselves, in a state of continual turmoil provoked by maltreatment at the hands of the Spaniards. They accordingly resolved to abandon their mission, and so the whole region was left without the light and staff of true doctrine, and the local people returned to the darkness and misery in which they had lived previously, deprived, at the very moment that they could most have used it and when they hungered after it, of the sovereign remedy that is knowledge of God, and left, for lack of spiritual sustenance, to wither as do seedlings when they are deprived of water. And all this was occasioned by the unforgivable behaviour and consummate wickedness of the Spaniards.

The natives of the province of Santa Marta had a great deal of gold, the province and its immediate neighbours being rich in the metal and the people who lived there having the will and the know-how to extract it. And this is the reason why, from 1498 right down to today, in 1542, the region has attracted an uninterrupted series of Spanish plunderers who have done nothing but sail there, attack, murder and rob the people, steal their gold and sail back again. Each expedition in turn – and there have been many over the years – has overrun the area, causing untold harm and a monstrous death-toll, and perpetrating countless atrocities. Until 1523, it was for the most part only the coastal strip that was blighted, and the countryside for a few leagues inland; but, in that year, a number of these Spanish brigands established a permanent settlement in the area and, since the region was, as we have said, extremely rich, that settlement witnessed the arrival of one commander after another, each set on outdoing his predecessor in villainy and cruelty, as though to prove the validity of the principle we outlined earlier.[99] The year 1529 saw the arrival of a considerable force under the command of one such Spaniard, a grimly determined individual, with no fear of God and not an ounce of compassion for his fellow-men; he proceeded to outshine all who had gone before him in the arts of terror, murder, and the most appalling cruelty. In the six or seven years he and his men were in the province,

98 Santa Marta was founded by Rodrigo de Bastidas in 1525 in what is now the Republic of Colombia
99 Alonso de Hojeda, Diego de Nicuesa, Vasco de Balboa, Pedrarias Dávila, García de Lerma, Pedro Fernández de Lugo, Alonso Luis de Lugo, etc. The 'principle' of which Las Casas speaks is set out on p. 25, above

they amassed a huge fortune. After his death – and he died without benefit of confession and in full flight from his official residence – there came other robbers and murderers who wiped out those of the local population who had survived the attentions of their predecessors. They extended their reign of terror far inland, plundering and devastating whole provinces, killing or capturing the people who lived there in much the same way as we have seen happening elsewhere, torturing chiefs and vassals alike in order to discover the whereabouts of the gold and, as we have said, far outdoing, in both quantity and quality, even the awfulness of those who had gone before them. This they did to such effect that they contrived to depopulate, between 1529 and today, an area of over four hundred leagues which was once as densely inhabited as any other.

I must confess that if I were to set down on paper each and every unforgivable violent crime committed against God, the King and the innocent people of the province by the Spanish in Santa Marta – every murder, every injustice, every atrocity, every attempt at genocide – they would make a very lengthy chronicle indeed. But that will be for the future, if the Lord spares me.[100] All I can do here is to quote a few words from a letter sent by the bishop of the province[101] to His Majesty the King. The letter bears the date 20 May 1541:

I submit, sacred Cæsar,[102] that the remedy for the ills that beset this territory is that Your Majesty remove from positions of authority the cruel usurpers presently in control and entrust it to someone who will love and care for it as he would his own offspring and will treat it properly as it deserves, and that Your Majesty attend to this as a

100 This is a reference to his *History of the Indies*; see Introduction, pp. xvii–xviii
101 Fray Juan Fernández de Ángulo. The practice of elevating members of the regular clergy to colonial bishoprics had grown up during the reign of Charles V
102 The Emperor Charles V was normally addressed as 'Cæsar'

81

matter of the highest priority. If nothing is done, I am certain that the whole territory will very soon simply disappear from the face of the earth, given the ways in which the cruel usurpers now maltreat and belabour it.

Further on in this same letter, the bishop writes:

It will be clear to Your Majesty from this how vital it is that those who presently govern these regions be stripped of their stewardship, so that the cruel yoke may be removed from the whole republic. If this is not done, I can see no remedy for the ills that now beset it. Your Majesty will also now perceive that here there are no Christians but only devils; no servants of God and the Crown but only traitors to His laws and Yours. It is my considered opinion that the greatest obstacle that stands in the way of the pacification of the New World, and with it the conversion of the people to Christ, is the harshness and cruelty of the treatment meted out by 'Christians' to those who surrender. This has been so harsh and so brutal that nothing is more odious nor more terrifying to the people than the name 'Christian', a word for which they use in their language the term *yares*, which means 'demons'. And such a usage is amply justified, for what has been done to them by the Spanish commanders and by their men has been neither Christian nor indeed the work of rational human beings, but rather the work of devils; and so, when the locals find themselves on the receiving end of such merciless butchery, they assume that such actions are standard among Christians and that they derive ultimately from a Christian God and a Christian King. Any attempt to persuade them otherwise is doomed to failure and quite understandably occasions snorts of derision, jibes about Christ and jeers at Him and His laws. The treatment of those who surrender only serves to confirm the belief of those who continue the struggle that it is better to die once and for all in battle than to suffer a thousand slow deaths at the hands of the Spanish. This, I know, Most Invincible Cæsar, from first-hand experience, etc.

And he goes on to say:

There are more servants of the Crown in these realms than Your Majesty may realize. For there is not a single soldier in the entire territory who does not declare openly, as he robs and plunders, as he murders or burns Your Majesty's subjects in order to get them to hand over gold, that he is doing so on Your Majesty's behalf and with Your Majesty's express authority. It would, therefore, be appropriate, Most Christian Cæsar, for Your Majesty to make it known, by the exemplary punishment of some of these culprits, that the Crown is not served by actions that are a disservice to God.

All this comes from an official report by the bishop of Santa Marta, and one can see clearly from it what is happening to these unfortunate territories and to their innocent inhabitants. When he speaks of those natives who 'continue the struggle' he means those who have managed to flee into the hills to escape butchery by Spanish scoundrels; and by those 'who surrender' he means those who, having survived the wholesale slaughter of their fellow-countrymen, now suffer the barbaric slavery to which the Spanish subject them and which we have already described – a slavery which will, as the bishop makes clear in his report, eventually prove fatal to each and every one of them. Indeed, he understates the horrific nature of the suffering to which they are subjected.

When they have been brought to the very edge of collapse by the labours to which they are put and begin to drop from hunger and toil as they stumble through the mountains with enormous loads on their backs, the Spaniards kick them and beat them with sticks to make them get up and resume their wearisome trudge. They do not allow them to stop and gasp for breath, and even knock their teeth out with the pommel of their swords. Their only response to such treatment is: 'I give up. You are evil and wicked. I cannot go on any longer. Kill me now. I do not want to live another moment.' This they say as they lie groaning and clutching their chests in what is clearly great agony.[103] Oh, would that I could describe even one hundredth part of the afflictions and calamities wrought among these innocent people by the benighted Spanish! May God grant enlightenment to those who are in a position to do something about what has been happening.

103 Many of the journeys described took place at high altitude

THE PROVINCE OF CARTAGENA

The province of Cartagena lies some fifty leagues down the coast to the west of Santa Marta. It shares a common frontier with the province of Cenú, extending as far as the Gulf of Urabá and forming a coastline which runs for some one hundred leagues. It also includes territory to the south extending inland for a great distance. These provinces have been persecuted, ravaged and cleared, and their people slaughtered from 1498 or 1499 right down to the present day just as has the province of Santa Marta.[104] They have witnessed barbaric atrocities and massacres by the Spanish, as well as plunder on the grand scale, but I shall not go into details here, as this is by way of a short account and I wish to move on to the mischief that is going on in other parts of the region.

104 Among those active in this region were Juan de la Cosa, Cristóbal Guerra, Alonso de Hojeda and Diego de Nicuesa

THE PEARL COAST, PARIA AND
TRINIDAD[105]

The whole of the area lying between the Paria and the Gulf of Venezuela, a distance of some two hundred leagues, has been the scene of wholesale destruction wrought upon the indigenous people by Spanish adventurers who have attacked them, taking as many as possible alive to sell as slaves. Often they have achieved this by deception, offering the people friendship and safe conduct and then going back on their word in a totally shameless fashion, even after the people have welcomed them into their homes as though they were long-lost brothers and done everything they possibly can for them. It would be imposs- ible to compile a detailed and accurate record of every instance of injustice, insult, harassment and outrage suffered by the people of the coast at the hands of the Spanish between 1510 and now, and I shall describe only two or three incidents as examples of countless such ugly atrocities, each and every one of them sufficient to earn the perpetrators the everlasting torment of Hell- fire.

The people who live on the island of Trinidad, which is both larger and more fertile than Sicily and lies just off the mainland close by Paria, are as good and virtuous as any to be found any- where in the New World. In 1516, one of these adventurers[106] made his way there with sixty or seventy men experienced in the

---

105 What Las Casas terms the 'Pearl Coast' and the 'Paria Coast' refer together to what is today known as the Paria Peninsula, in northeast Venezuela. The pearl- fishing was conducted in the waters around the Isla Margarita (literally, 'Pearl Island')

106 Juan Bono. Las Casas, *History of the Indies*, book III, chapter 91, says no more than that Bono was a Basque, remarking sourly that he was as good (*bono*) as the negro Juan Blanco – a famous pirate and despoiler of the Amerindians – was white (*blanco*)

ways of robbery and announced that he and his men were coming to settle on the island and to live alongside the native people. The locals welcomed them as though they were their own flesh and blood, both the chief and the people dancing attendance upon them, showing every sign of joy and affection, and bringing them every single day twice as much food as they could possibly eat. Indeed, the indigenous peoples of the New World are by nature extremely generous and, in their rush to provide the Spanish with more than they need, often hand over everything they possess. They built a large wooden house big enough for all the members of the Spanish expedition to live in, since the Spaniards insisted on being quartered together in order that they might carry out the plan they had hatched. Once the wooden framework of the house was complete, work began on thatching the structure. As soon as the walls were finished to more than twice the height of a man and those inside the building could no longer see what was going on outside, the Spanish made a great pretence of wanting to finish the job as quickly as possible and packed a very large number of men inside the building. They then took their arms and deployed themselves around the outside of the house to seal off all the exits, and also stationed a number of men inside the building itself. Those inside then drew their swords and instructed the naked and defenceless natives to stand perfectly still, threatening to kill them if they did not. They next began to tie them up, while those that tried to escape were hacked to pieces by the guards stationed outside. A few did manage to get away, although some were wounded in the process, and regrouped in another building, joining forces with those locals who had not been in the new house during the attack. Here they set about defending themselves as best they could with bows and arrows. There were between a hundred and two hundred of them, but the Spanish posted men on the doors to prevent any escape and then set fire to the building, burning them alive, before making for their ship, taking with them a prize consisting of the one hundred and eighty to two hundred men they had seized and bound at the outset and, setting sail for Puerto Rico, they sold half of the consignment there as slaves before sailing on to Hispaniola where they sold the rest. When I was on the island of Puerto Rico and had the opportunity to confront this particular commander with his wicked behaviour and with having betrayed these people, his reply was: 'Come off it, Sir. The orders I had from my superiors were quite specific: if I could not capture them in battle, I was to promise them peace as a way of tricking them into giving themselves up, and then enslave them.' When, in conversation, he admitted the enormity of his crimes and the shame he felt about them, he confessed that he had never felt more at home than he had on the island of Trinidad and that the local people had treated him as one of their own and had done everything they could for him. Yet incidents like this, in which local people have been lured into giving themselves up by promises that no harm will be done to them, have been commonplace enough on the mainland, and one is left to judge for oneself the justice of such a method of enslaving natives.

On another occasion, the Dominicans, our own Order, decided to mount a mission to bring the Word of Christ to the peoples of the New World because they were ignorant of the truth and were accordingly (and still are) in mortal danger of being denied the Life Everlasting. It was decided to send among them a monk, a man of great virtue and holiness and fully versed in theology, and he was to have a lay brother as his companion.[107] The idea was that they should get to know the lie of the land and make contact with local people with a view to deciding where best to establish monasteries. The people received them as angels from Heaven, listening with rapt attention and great emotion and joy to what they had to say, even though this had to be conveyed by

---

107 See Las Casas, *History of the Indies*, book III, chapters 4 and 39. Francisco Hernández de Córdoba O.P. was one of the companions of Antonio Montesinos
(see Introduction, pp. xx–xxi); Juan Garcés, like Las Casas himself, had been an
encomendero before his conversion to the Amerindian cause.

sign and gesture as the Dominicans did not speak the local language. After the ship which had brought the missionaries had sailed away another vessel arrived. The Dominicans were not aware of it at the time, but the Spaniards invited the local chief on board this vessel together with a hundred of his men, ostensibly for a party.[108] This local chief, who was known as Alonso (presumably a name given him by the Spaniards or by the missionaries, local people being very keen to acquire a Christian name and often asking for one even before they are taught the rudiments of Christianity necessary for baptism), would not normally have trusted such an invitation but he was tricked into a false sense of security by the presence of the Dominicans, believing that the Spaniards would not do him any harm all the time the missionaries were there. He, his wife and seventeen others went on board, but no sooner had they done so than the ship set sail for Hispaniola where the hostages were sold into slavery. The people, seeing their chief and his wife carried off in this manner, were minded to execute the missionaries in return, and the missionaries themselves were mortified at the wickedness shown by the Spanish, for they would have died rather than countenance such treachery, especially as they sensed it would prove a real obstacle to the conversion of the people. They did their best to mollify them, assuring them that they would send word to Hispaniola by the first available vessel and would contrive to ensure the safe return of the chief and those who were with him. As God would have it, a vessel did arrive and with it an opportunity to confirm the perfidy of those in authority throughout the region. For the Dominicans duly wrote to their fellow-missionaries on Hispaniola, protesting repeatedly about this treachery, only for it soon to become plain that the magistrates there had no intention of investigating the case because they had themselves received a number of the slaves

108 There is a more detailed account of this episode in Las Casas, *History of the Indies*, book III, chapter 33

taken in this evil and criminal fashion. Once the two who had made the original promise that chief Alonso and his companions would be back safe and sound within four months saw no sign of this happening four or even eight months later, they prepared to meet their fate and to give their lives for the Lord to whom they had pledged themselves before setting out on their mission. And so it was that the local people exacted their revenge, executing two innocent men. Yet they did so justly according to their own lights, for they thought the missionaries had been party to the act of treachery, the missionaries' solemn promise had not been honoured, and they no more knew then than they do now that there is a distinction between monks on the one hand and the Spanish robbers, bandits, and tyrants who roam the territory on the other. These blessed brothers were the victims of injustice and, as such, there can be no doubt that they are true and blessed martyrs of the faith nor that they are now united with God in the kingdom of Heaven, having done their duty on earth as enjoined by the vow of obedience and having laboured as instructed to spread the Gospel, to save the souls of all the peoples of the region, and to suffer in the name of the crucified Christ whatever trials and whatever destiny should befall them.

On yet another occasion, which I witnessed at first hand as only by a miracle did I escape the same fate, local people killed two other Dominicans and a Franciscan.[109] Once again, this horrendous incident was sparked off by the wickedness of Christians and it proved sufficiently grave to shock the whole world. But in this brief account I shall not dwell upon it[110], but rather wait until the Day of Judgement when all shall be made clear and God will come to punish the wickedness and atrocious behaviour towards the inhabitants of the New World of men masquerading as Christians.

---

109 This occurred during the abortive attempt by Francisco de Soto to colonize Cumaná in January 1522
110 See Las Casas, *History of the Indies*, book III, chapter 159

Another incident occurred in this same area, at Codera Point, where stood a town whose chief was known as Higoroto, which was either the chief's own name or possibly a title given to all the lords in the area in question.[111] The chief himself was a goodly man and his people so virtuous that a Spaniard putting in there could be sure to find food and rest, and an opportunity to relax and recuperate. Indeed, many Spaniards who fetched up there, dropping from exhaustion and hunger in their headlong rush to escape from other parts of the country that they had made too hot for themselves by their atrocities and excesses, and whom he could have quietly despatched without anyone being any the wiser, were instead given food and safe passage to Margarita Island where there was a Christian garrison. In short, the town of Higueroto was known to all the Europeans as every man's hostel and every man's home. The local people had no apparent reason to be on their guard against anybody and, because of this, one Spanish adventurer[112] decided they would be easy game. He sailed in and issued a general invitation for the locals to come aboard his ship, which was something they were used to doing when Spanish vessels were in port. With many of them – men, women and children – safely on board, he set sail for Puerto Rico, where he sold them all into slavery. When I myself arrived in Puerto Rico, I met this Spanish captain and learned in detail of what he had done. He was responsible for the destruction of the entire town, an abomination which gave rise to great consternation among the Spanish adventurers operating in the area, all of whom looked upon it as a safe refuge and a home from home.

I repeat that many similar atrocities and countless acts of wickedness will here pass unremarked, even though they continue unabated to the present day.

111 The modern town of Higuerote lies to the south of Codera Point (*Cabo Codera*) and some sixty miles east of Caracas. The discrepancy in the spelling is in the original

112 See Las Casas, *History of the Indies*, book III, chapter 166

From what was once the heavily populated coastal area of the Paria Peninsula, over two million souls have been kidnapped and taken to the islands of Hispaniola and Puerto Rico to be sent down the mines or put to other work. There, as did those of whom we spoke earlier, they perished in droves. It is a heart-rending sight to travel along that coast, once so fertile and so populous, and to see it as it is today, totally abandoned and left to go to rack and ruin.

It is a fact beyond dispute that whenever one of these vessels sets sail, loaded to the gunwales with natives who have been rounded up and forcibly embarked, at least a third of the poor wretches perish during the voyage and are thrown overboard, and one has also to remember that many are killed before they ever get as far as the ships. The reason the death-toll is so high is that, in order to maximize profits, the men who finance these slave-fleets arrange for the vessels to carry nothing in the way of victuals except a basic minimum for the crew and so there is hardly any food or water for the poor prisoners who, as a consequence, perish from thirst and hunger and are consigned to a watery grave. One witness told me personally that, on a voyage from the Bahamas, where many natives had been rounded up, to Hispaniola, a distance of sixty or seventy leagues, one vessel, which was navigating without a compass and with no chart of the region, kept its course only by reference to the string of dead bodies wallowing in its wake.

Later, the spectacle of these poor creatures disembarked on the island where they are to be sold is enough to break the heart of anyone with a spark of human feeling. They are naked, and so weakened by hunger that many – old and young alike, men and women – simply drop where they stand. Then they are split up into groups of between ten and twenty, like so many sheep being driven to market: a parent is parted from a child, a woman from her husband; and lots are cast as a way of apportioning the little flocks between the wretched *armadores* (the individuals who originally pooled resources to charter the two or three vessels

that make up the slave convoy) and those who actually sa
the native villages and took part in the round-up itself. If
finds himself allotted a flock in which there is an old man or in
which someone is sickly, his response is normally: 'To the Devil
with this old man. Why make me take him? I suppose you want
me to bury him? Why should I take this sickly one? Am I to
waste my substance on curing him?' Reactions like these serve
to give some idea of what the Spanish think of the native
people, and how closely they obey that commandment to
love one's neighbour that underpins the Law and the books
of the Prophets.

One of the cruellest and most damnable things in the whole of
Creation is the way in which the Spanish use natives to fish for
pearls. The life of a pearl-fisher in these conditions is worse than
any other on the face of the earth; it is even more dreadful and
more terrible than that of the native gold-miner, ghastly though
that undoubtedly is. They are in the water from dawn to dusk,
often operating at depths of four and five fathoms. Seldom are
they permitted to surface for air but must spend their time
swimming under water and tearing at the oysters in which pearls
grow. Once they have filled their nets they surface, gasping, and
hand the oysters to the Spanish taskmaster who sits in a smack
or a canoe. If they spend more than a few seconds at the surface
to get their breath back, he will punch them or grab them by the
hair and push them back under, making them dive once more.
Their only food is fish – and then only oysters – plus, perhaps,
some cassava bread (they bake with cassava flour throughout the
region), the oysters providing little in the way of sustenance and
the cassava being extremely hard to make.[113] They are kept
perpetually hungry. At night, they are shackled to prevent them
from escaping and have to sleep on the hard ground. Often,
when out fishing or searching for pearls, a man will dive never

---

113 The making of flour from the roots of the cassava (*caçabí*, in Old Spanish),
   widely grown throughout the region, was a complex process involving the
   removal of poisonous juices

to resurface, for the poor wretches are easy prey to all manner of sharks, those most ferocious of marine creatures, capable of swallowing a man whole. One can see just how closely the greed of those Spaniards involved in this profitable enterprise of pearl-fishing induces obedience to God's commandment to love Him and to love one's neighbour, for they place their fellow-creatures in peril of both body and soul (the wretches dying without learning of Christ and without the benefit of the Sacraments). On top of this, their victims are forced to spend their last days in agony, and the nature of the work is such that they perish in any case within a few days, for no man can spend long under water without coming up for air, and the water is so cold that it chills them to the marrow. Most choke on their own blood as the length of time they must stay under water without breathing and the attendant pressure upon their lungs makes them haemorrhage from the mouth; others are carried off by dysentery caused by the extreme cold to which they are subjected. Their hair, which is naturally jet black, takes on a singed appearance more typical of sea-wolves, and their backs come out in great salt sores, so that they look more like deformed monsters than men, or like members of another species altogether. By condemning them to this quite unbearable toil – or, to put it more accurately, this living Hell – the oppressors have exterminated the entire population of the Bahamas, not a single soul living there when the Spanish first discovered this trade having survived. The pearl-divers fetch fifty or a hundred *castilians* on the open market because of the great skill of Bahamians as swimmers and they are sold despite an unusually enlightened ban on these auctions issued by the justices. The pearl fisheries have been the grave of countless non-Bahamians also, drafted in from other parts of the New World.

THE RIVER YUYAPARÍ

Through the province of Paria runs the river Yuyaparí, which extends upstream more than two hundred leagues. In 1529, one of these miserable adventurers made his way many leagues upstream together with four hundred or so of his men. There they found people living quietly in their homes and on their lands, and doing harm to nobody. Among these innocents, they proceeded to create mayhem, killing large numbers of them, burning them alive and putting them to the sword; their lands destroyed, the people abandoned much of the territory in their terror. Eventually, this villain came to a sticky end and his fleet was dispersed; but others came after him, ravaging the land, killing the people and despatching to Hell these poor souls for whom the Son of God died on the Cross.

THE KINGDOM OF VENEZUELA

It has become the custom to falsify reports sent back to Spain about the damaging nature of Spanish actions in the New World, the harm it does to the indigenous peoples, and its disservice to the Christian cause and to the Crown. In 1526, a series of such misleading reports induced the Crown, as part of a treaty or deal which they were then concluding, to place under the jurisdiction of German merchants, wholly and unconditionally, a great kingdom, known as Venezuela and far larger than Spain itself.[114] When the merchants arrived in the region, with at least three hundred men under their command, they found a people even more docile than those encountered on previous expeditions to other parts of the New World (before, that is, Spanish depredations altered everything irrevocably). In my opinion, the Venezuela expedition was incomparably more barbaric than any we have so far described, and the men involved in it more inhumane and more vicious than savage tigers, more ferocious than lions or than ravening wolves. Fear of God, duty to the Crown and respect for their fellow-men were all discarded in their blind and obsessive greed, and they went further than any of their predecessors in devising new and ever more refined methods of cruelty and duplicity to obtain the gold and silver they craved, behaving as absolute dictators of the territory, and with not a thought for their own souls.

These devils in human form have been responsible for devastating over four hundred leagues of the most fertile and blessed

114 The deal, signed in the spring of 1528 (not 1526) with the Welser banking house of Augsburg, was to have important implications for the slave trade. Welser agents in Venezuela included Heinrich Ehiger, Hieronymus Sieler, Ambrosius Eingher (or Alfinger), Georg Spier and Nikolaus Federmann

land on earth, and for killing all the people or driving them out of great provinces that once struck awe in the beholder: valleys forty leagues in extent, whole regions as delightful as one could desire and settlements as rich in gold as they were populous. They have annihilated entire nations, and with these people have disappeared a multitude of languages that are no longer spoken save perhaps by a few individuals living in remote caves in the bowels of the earth whither they have fled to escape the pestilential sword hanging over them. My own estimate is that over four or five million of these poor souls have been despatched to the depths of Hell by these fiends with their capacity for inventing diabolical and ever more sadistic methods of mass murder. The carnage continues unabated even as I write. Of the countless cases of injustice on the grand scale, and of atrocities past and present, I should like to cite just three or four which will give some idea of the lengths to which these men are prepared to go to satisfy their lust for pillage and bloodshed.

Without any provocation, they seized the king of the whole province and set about wringing gold out of him by torture. He escaped and fled to the mountains in open revolt against his tormentors; throughout the territory the people were absolutely terrified and went into hiding in the mountains and in the surrounding countryside. The Spaniards mounted expeditions to hunt them down and, when they found them, killed many, auctioning the survivors as slaves. Before they seized the king, wherever they ventured throughout the territory the Spaniards had been warmly welcomed with singing and dancing, and with many unsolicited gifts of gold. In return, the Spaniards set about terrorizing the entire province by slitting the throats of their benefactors and dismembering them with their swords. On one occasion, one of these German blackguards forced a crowd of locals, who had come to greet him in the manner we have described, into a large building made of thatch and then ordered his men to cut them to pieces. Some of those inside managed to clamber on to the roof-beams of the building in an attempt to place themselves beyond the reach of the bloodthirsty brutes who were mercilessly belabouring the crowd with their swords; but this hellhound gave orders for the building to be fired and those that had escaped the mayhem going on below were burned alive. Many towns and settlements were abandoned as the local people, learning of this massacre, fled to the hills in an attempt to escape such butchery.

In another large province, on the borders of the kingdom of Santa Marta, the local people were going about their usual business at home and in the fields when the Europeans arrived. For a time, the visitors graciously allowed the natives to treat them as honoured guests and to dance attendance upon them as if they were about to have eternal life bestowed upon them by these gods. During this period the poor people patiently bore the many indignities and intolerable burdens which the European presence imposed upon them, for one of these newcomers will wolf down in one day enough food and drink to support a local family of ten for a whole month. The people also regaled the Europeans with many gifts of gold as well as doing them innumerable other services. When the time came for the tyrants to leave, they elected to pay for their board and lodging in the following way. The German governor – who was anyway, in my opinion, a heretic, never going himself to Mass, preventing others from doing so and giving other indications of Protestantism[115] – ordered that as many of the locals as possible should be seized, including women and children, and driven into a stockade which he had built expressly for this purpose. He then let it be known that the prisoners would only be released if they arranged for a ransom to be paid directly to the unspeakable governor: so much for a man, and then so much for his wife and so much for each child. To ensure that his victims were responsive to his

---

115 The Spanish term employed by Las Casas, *luterano* (strictly speaking, 'Lutheran'), was widely used, both in Europe and the New World, to indicate any deviant from the prevailing Catholic religious orthodoxy

demands, he also decreed that no prisoner should be fed until his or her ransom had been paid. Many of the prisoners sent home for gold and, if they could raise the necessary ransom, paid it and promptly set off home in search of food and expecting to resume their normal lives. The villain then sent a number of his hoodlums to seize the poor devils and throw them back into the stockade where they were forced to endure all over again the miseries of thirst and hunger until they were ransomed a second time. Many were released and re-imprisoned two or three times, while others, who could not raise the price asked, because they had already parted with all the gold in their possession, were simply left in the stockade to die of hunger.

In this fashion a whole province, once populous and rich in gold, was devastated, ravaged and depopulated. In the valley, some forty leagues in extent, a whole settlement of a thousand houses was razed to the ground.

This same hellhound then decided to strike inland, his insatiable appetite whetted by the prospect of an overland route to the Hell that is Peru. On this dreadful journey he took with him a vast number of native bearers, shackled together and each weighed down by a load of three or four *arrobas*.[116] Whenever one of these poor wretches fainted from hunger or became too exhausted to carry on, they cut his head from his body at the point where the iron collar bound him to his companions, so as not to have to waste time unshackling him from the bearers to either side of him; his head would fall to one side and his decapitated body to the other, and his load would then be distributed among his fellows, adding to their already heavy burdens. To set out in detail the vast tracts of land he ravaged, the towns and villages he burned to the ground (for all the houses are built of thatch), the people he slaughtered and the atrocities he committed *en route*, in place after place, would be to produce an account that nobody would believe, only too

116 See above, p. 24, note 32

terribly true though it would be. Other adventurers from Venezuela and Santa Marta were to pass that way on their holy pilgrimage to the golden shrine of Peru, and even they, seasoned campaigners that they were, were shocked and appalled by the grim trail of destruction blazed by this butcher over a distance of two hundred leagues and more, turning what had been a fertile and populated area into one vast, scorched wasteland.

Witnesses to all these events have given evidence before the legal adviser to the Council of the Indies, and the Council now has incontrovertible proof of the truth of their allegations. Yet not one single hellhound has been burned at the stake. Indeed, the justices have proved unpardonably deaf to the many accounts placed before them of the atrocities perpetrated by these foul and despicable murderers and the damage they have done. Ignoring the crimes themselves, they concentrate their attention instead on assessing the financial losses incurred by the Crown as a result of the atrocities and massacres carried out by the individuals identified by witnesses. In arriving at estimates of this kind, reliable eye-witness accounts are totally discounted; all that seems to be required is a general statement of what has taken place, and such general statements tend to be hazy and unspecific. The justices seem not to know how to investigate even the financial aspect of these atrocities at all accurately or professionally; if they did so, as conscientious servants of God and the Crown, they would quickly discover that these German villains have embezzled Crown revenues to the tune of over three million gold *castilians*. For the provinces of Venezuela, together with the more than four hundred leagues of territory totally devastated and ruined in the way we have seen, formed the most heavily populated area on earth as well as the most prosperous and the richest in gold. And, over the sixteen years that have elapsed since these foul enemies of God and the Crown first began their depredations, they have been responsible for losses to the Treasury amounting to more than the total official returns from the entire kingdom, which stand at some two million gold *castilians*.

And there is no hope that losses on this scale can ever be recouped, unless God should at some future date be pleased to resurrect many millions of souls. But these are only the temporal losses to the Crown. It is time we stopped to reflect on the other costs: the blasphemous and dishonourable outrages committed against God and against divine law, and the countless souls, now beyond redemption, who burn in everlasting Hell as a direct result of the greed and the inhumanity of these Swabian – or, more properly, swinish – butchers. [117]

My last observation on the savagery of these brutes is this. Over the sixteen years since first they arrived in the region, they have sent shipload after shipload of natives for sale in Santa Marta or on the islands of Hispaniola, Jamaica and Puerto Rico. In all they must have despatched more than a million of them in this way, and the traffic is still going on today, in 1542, with the royal *Audiencia* of Hispaniola, which could easily put a stop to it, turning a blind eye to what is going on and, indeed, aiding and abetting it, as it has over the years condoned other atrocious practices which have been current in the over four hundred leagues of mainland coastal territory in Venezuela and Santa Marta under its jurisdiction. The only reason for enslaving these natives is the perverse, stubborn and purblind willingness of officials to pander to the insatiable appetite for money shown by these greedy villains – an appetite which has reared its head at every turn and which has led to adventurers of this type throughout the New World using every trick in the book and sparing no form of cruelty to lead these docile people into slavery, like lambs to the slaughter, and branding them, their wives and their children with the King's mark.

117 The pun in Spanish is: *'animales o alemanes'* (animals or Germans)

Since 1510 or 1511 three tyrannical adventurers have made their way to these provinces and behaved in much the same way as have their compatriots in other parts of the New World. Two of them already had blood on their hands from campaigns in other parts of the region,[118] and had clawed their way up to their present commands not on merit but over the dead bodies of their fellow-men. I knew them personally, and all three came to a sticky end, the fortunes they amassed by pillage and murder have long since been dispersed and all memory of them has been expunged from the face of the earth. It is now as though they had never been born. Yet, during their lifetime, the whole world was struck dumb with terror at the mere mention of their names and at reports of the killings for which they were responsible; not that, in the end, there were all that many of these, for the Lord was quick to bring them to account for the crimes I had seen them commit in other parts of the New World, cutting them short before they could wreak havoc on a larger scale in these provinces. A fourth and very determined blackguard arrived in the area far more recently, in 1538.[119] He came with a large force fully prepared for the campaign he had in mind, but has since disappeared and it is now three years since anyone has seen him or had word of him. Yet there is no doubt that he will have set about tyrannizing the people as soon as he arrived in the region, nor that, if he is still alive, he will have murdered anyone and everyone unlucky enough to cross his path, for he is a notoriously ruthless and seasoned campaigner

118 Probably Ponce de León and Pánfilo de Narváez. See above, pp. 29 and 48
119 Hernando de Soto, who died in the area in 1542 or 1543

and he and his companions-in-arms have been responsible for some of the worst atrocities ever seen in the New World. It is my belief that God has already called him to account as He did those who preceded him.

Some three or four years since the above was written, the survivors of this last expedition re-emerged into public view. Their leader did, indeed, meet his end in Florida, but the brutes who were with him were able to give us an account of the dreadful atrocities he and, after his miserable death, they committed among the poor, harmless natives – atrocities which fully justify the assessment given above. Their account of the Florida expedition underlines the general principle I enunciated earlier: that the longer men have operated in the New World and the more they have become accustomed to the carnage and butchery around them, the more brutal and the more wicked have been the crimes they commit against God and their fellow-men.[120] We have had a bellyful of describing the horrible, bloody and disgusting deeds of individuals such as these, wild beasts rather than human beings, and so I shall give details of the following incidents only.

On their travels, they encountered great settlements whose inhabitants were handsome and intelligent and who lived in well-ordered and structured societies. They murdered many (as is their custom) in order to strike terror into the hearts of these people. They made their lives an utter misery, treating them as so many beasts of burden. As we have already related, whenever one of these unfortunates became so weary he could no longer stagger on, they simply sliced his head from his shoulders so they would not have to stop to break the chains around his neck, and his head would fall to one side of the baggage train and his trunk to the other.

In one town, the people received them joyfully and set before them a huge banquet, far more than they could eat. They also

120 See above, p. 25

offered six hundred of their own men as bearers and to act as grooms for the horses. After the Spaniards had taken their leave, one of the captains, a kinsman of the commander, returned to the town, now basking in the mistaken belief that it was safe from attack, and plundered it, skewering the local leader and king of the entire region on the point of his lance and committing many other acts of brutality.

In another large town, the local people were, it would seem, a little more cautious on account of rumours they had heard of atrocities perpetrated elsewhere by the Spaniards; this the butchers used as a pretext to put the whole town to the sword, young and old, chiefs and commoners. Not even the children were spared.

It is reported that the butcher-in-chief arranged for a large number of natives in the area and, in particular, one group of over two hundred who had either come from a neighbouring town in response to a summons or had gathered of their own free will, to have their noses, lips and chins sliced from their faces; they were then sent away, in unspeakable agony and all running with blood, to act as walking testimony to the great deeds and holy miracles performed by these dauntless missionaries of the Holy Catholic Faith. The reader can judge for himself the reaction of the local people to such messengers, their great love of Christians, their certainty of the goodness and justice of the Lord, and how pure they must think the law and religion professed with pride by disciples such as these. The wickedness of such men, who have sold their souls to the Devil, knows no bounds and their deeds beggar belief. Their wretched leader died a wretched death without benefit of confession, and there can be no doubt that he is now in the depths of Hell enjoying the wages of his wickedness; unless, that is, he has been sentenced not according to his own just deserts but according to the Lord's divine mercy.

THE RIVER PLATE

Since 1522 or 1523, there have been three or four expeditions that have made their way to the river Plate, a region of great kingdoms and provinces, where dwell many handsome and intelligent peoples.[121] We know that these expeditions have occasioned many deaths and that a great deal of harm has been done generally to the people living in the area, but, given that the region is very remote from the rest of the New World, available details are few and far between. Yet we have no reservation in stating that this region has experienced and continues to experience outrages of the kind that have occurred throughout the New World because the adventurers are Spaniards, and many are veterans of other campaigns of brutality, hell-bent on amassing private fortunes and becoming men of consequence as have others of their compatriots, and this they could not achieve without going in for the plunder, murder and perverse degradation of the native population that has characterized Spanish action in other parts of the continent.

After the above was written, reliable news arrived that these men have indeed waged a campaign of plunder and destruction on the grand scale throughout this region. They have taxed their own powers of invention in devising new ways to torture and murder their luckless victims; indeed, because the region is so remote from Spain and so inaccessible, they have had fewer restraints on their actions and have, if anything, behaved even more wretchedly and unjustly than their compatriots operating in other parts of the New World, terrible though the record of

121 The region, discovered in 1515 by Díaz de Solís, was the object of expeditions by, among others, Sebastian Cabot, Pedro de Mendoza, Martínez de Irala, Juan de Ayolas and Álvar Núñez Cabeza de Vaca

those other expeditions has been, as we know full well from what has been recorded so far.

Among other atrocities reported to the Council of the Indies are the following. One of the governing despots ordered a number of his men to take themselves off to certain local native settlements and, should they not be offered hospitality, massacre the entire population. In the event, the people, who viewed them as enemies and were scared stiff of coming to close quarters with them, offered nothing and, following their instructions to the letter, the Spaniards put over five thousand souls to the sword.

On another occasion, a number of natives who had already acknowledged Spanish dominion came to offer service to these petty tyrants, possibly in response to a summons. And, either because they did not come quickly enough when called, or simply because to do so had become second nature, it was decided to terrorize them and the order went out that they were to be handed over to another local tribe with whom they were at war. The hapless victims wept and implored the villains to kill them on the spot rather than deliver them to their enemies and cowered in the building where they had taken shelter, refusing to come out. There they were hacked to pieces, even as they shouted and wailed: 'We came in peace to serve you and you kill us; may our blood on these walls serve as testimony to your cruelty and to the injustice of our deaths.' This was indeed a dreadful and lamentable outrage.

THE GREAT KINGDOMS AND PROVINCES
OF PERU

In 1531 another great villain journeyed with a number of men to the kingdoms of Peru.[122] He set out with every intention of imitating the strategy and tactics of his fellow-adventurers in other parts of the New World (and he had a great deal of experience of the New World, having played a full part over a number of years in the atrocities and barbarities that had been happening on the Mainland ever since 1510), but, as time went on, his cruelty came to outstrip even that of his predecessors, as he criminally murdered and plundered his way through the region, razing towns and cities to the ground and slaughtering and otherwise tormenting in the most barbaric fashion imaginable the people who lived there. Throughout the territory, his wickedness was on such a scale that nobody will ever really learn the full extent of it until all is revealed on the Day of Judgement. Indeed, it would be impossible to depict in all their ugly and horrendous detail the outrages and atrocities I shall now describe.

His first act on entering the territory was to sack a number of towns and steal a huge quantity of gold from them. When he visited the island of Puná[123] which lies just off the coast of the province, the lord and the people of this beautiful and populous island welcomed him and his men as though they were angels come from Heaven. Yet, after six months, the visitors had consumed everything there was to eat and all that remained were the supplies of maize the people had laid in to feed themselves

---

122 Francisco Pizarro
123 The island, given by Las Casas as 'Pugna', lies off the coast of Ecuador in the Gulf of Guayaquil

and their families should there be a drought or should the harvest fail. Even these, and with tears in their eyes, they freely offered to their guests. The way the guests repaid this hospitality was to set about them with sword and lance, killing many and enslaving the rest, treating them the while in the most barbaric and cruel fashion. As a result, the island has been all but depopulated.

They then travelled on to the province of Tumbes[124] on the mainland where they smashed everything in sight and killed everyone they could lay their hands on. And, when the people all fled before them because of the horrendous acts of atrocity they were committing, they proclaimed them rebels against the Spanish Crown. The method favoured by this butcher was this: when people brought him gifts of gold and silver, or when he himself demanded they should do so, he would insist on their bringing more and more, until he convinced himself that they either had no more to bring or would refuse to produce anything further. He then solemnly declared them subjects of the Spanish Crown, embraced them and got two of his men to sound the trumpet by way of indicating that from now on they were entitled to protection and need surrender no further goods, thus conveniently discounting the thefts that had already taken place and ignoring the 'gifts' which, because of his terrifying reputation, the natives had made to him before he had extended royal protection to them. This was all done as though the crimes committed already – the thefts, the oppression, the sacking of their towns and cities – had not been perpetrated under the aegis of the Spanish Crown and as though he personally had had no hand in them.

A few days later he and his men had a visit from the king and emperor of the entire territory, who was called Atahualpa.[125] He came accompanied by many of his men, all naked and armed,

---

124 In northwest Peru, Las Casas giving this as 'Tumbala', possibly as a result of confusion with the name of the cacique of Puná
125 Consistently called by Las Casas 'Atabaliba'

though their arms were a joke because they had never felt the edge of a sword nor the point of a lance. They were ignorant of the true nature of these Spaniards (who would attack and rob the Devil himself if he had gold about his person) and had never witnessed the speed of their horses. As soon as Atahualpa approached, he cried: 'Where are these Spaniards? Let them come out at once, for I shall not leave without satisfaction for the murder of my subjects, the destruction of my towns and cities and the wealth they have stolen from me.' The Spaniards duly came out, seized the king, who was carried on a kind of litter, and killed vast numbers of the men who were with him. They then haggled with him over the ransom to be paid for his release. He agreed to the sum of four million *castilians*, and in the event paid fifteen, and they agreed to release him. But, in the end, they did not honour their side of the bargain (for nowhere in the New World did the Spanish keep their word) but falsely accused him of ordering his people to assemble. His reply was that throughout his realm not a single leaf on a single tree stirred without his express permission, and if the people had assembled, it must indeed be because he had instructed them to do so; now that the Spanish had him in their clutches, they would be well advised to kill him. In spite of such a spirited response, they decided they would burn him alive, although several Spaniards did later ask their commander to throttle him before he was burned, and in the event he was throttled and then burned. Once he learned of his fate, he asked them: 'Why do you want to burn me? What harm have I done you? Did you not give your word that you would let me go if I gave you gold? Did I not give you all I promised and more? If you do not wish to free me, then send me to your King of Spain.' These and the other things he said sprang from his anger and from the fury he felt at the injustice that was being done him. But they burned him all the same. This episode, with its imprisonment of that great lord, his sentence and execution, reveals only too clearly the pretext upon which this 'just war' was conducted and the clear consciences with which these adventurers amassed huge personal fortunes in this part of the world by robbing him and sundry other lords and private individuals.

Of the many wicked and barbarous atrocities committed by those calling themselves Christians in their determination to root out and exterminate these peoples, I shall now relate one or two that were witnessed in the early days by a Franciscan friar who sent sworn and signed testimony of what happened both to the local authorities and back home to Spain.[126] I have in my possession a copy of his testimony, signed in his own hand, which reads:

I, Brother Marcos de Niza, of the Order of St Francis, Commissioner for the provinces of Peru of the said Order, being one of the very first religious to set foot in these provinces, hereby bear true witness of certain things which I have seen for myself in the territory in question, touching in particular the treatment and conquest of the indigenous peoples of the region. I have first-hand experience of these peoples and can state unequivocally and without fear of contradiction that the inhabitants of Peru are the best disposed of all the indigenous people of the New World towards the Europeans and have always treated them with openness and friendship. They bestowed upon them princely gifts of gold, silver, and precious stones, and handed over whatever the Spanish asked of them as well as doing them every service. The people never attacked the Spanish but, until the Spaniards began to maltreat them so cruelly, always behaved towards them in peace and with friendship, welcoming them publicly wherever they went, mounting banquets in their honour, and presenting them with as many slaves as the Spanish desired, both men and women.

126 Fray Marcos's accusations were originally made in a letter to the bishop of Mexico, the Franciscan Juan de Zumárraga

I, being an eye-witness to these events, hereby testify that, after the great cacique Atahualpa had given them over two million in gold[127] and surrendered all the lands under his jurisdiction without any resistance whatever, the Spaniards did, without any provocation whatever on the part of the native people, burn the said Atahualpa, lord of the entire kingdom, and then straight away did burn alive his captain-general Chalcuchima, who had, with other leading citizens of the kingdom, come in peace to greet the Spanish governor. In the same fashion they did, within the space of a few days, burn another blameless leader, the lord of Quito province, one Chamba, without even troubling to produce a pretext for doing so. Equally without cause did they burn Chapera, lord of the Cañari.[128] They burned the feet of Alvis, a great lord from Quito, and tortured him in various other ways to get him to reveal the whereabouts of Atahualpa's treasure, of which (it would seem) he knew nothing. In Quito, the governor of all the provinces of Quito,[129] who had come in peace in response to a request from Sebastián de Benalcázar,[130] commander-in-chief to the governor, was burned alongside many other caciques and leading citizens because the gold he handed over did not match the sum demanded of him. My own belief is that the Spanish plan was to ensure that they did away with all the local lords bar none throughout the entire territory.

I testify that the Spaniards gathered a considerable number of local people and locked up as many of them as they could fit into three large buildings to which they set light, burning

---

127 It is not clear whether this figure is meant to indicate two million *castilians* (see above, p. 19, note 19) or a similar number of *pesos*

128 A people of southern central Ecuador

129 This is probably the person the royal chronicler Antonio de Herrera calls 'Zope-Zopahua'. He had, in fact, been leader of the opposition to Sebastián de Benalcázar in the Quito region

130 Benalcázar was the conqueror of Nicaragua and one of the members of Pizarro's first expedition

The Spaniards ... seized the king ... and killed vast members of the men who were with him.

to death those inside even though they had done absolutely nothing whatever to merit such treatment. On that occasion a priest, one Ocaña, managed to get one lad out of the burning building but a Spaniard came and took the boy from him and thrust him back into the inferno where he was burned to a cinder along with all the rest. Later that day, this same Spaniard dropped dead on his way back to camp and I was of the opinion that he should be refused a Christian burial.

I testify that I saw with my own eyes Spaniards cutting off the hands, noses and ears of local people, both men and women, simply for the fun of it, and that this happened time and again in various places throughout the region. On several occasions I also saw them set dogs on the people, many being torn to pieces in this fashion, and they also burned down houses and even whole settlements, too numerous to count. It is also the case that they tore babes and sucklings from the mother's breast and played games with them, seeing who could throw them the farthest. I was a witness to other outrages and to hair-raising barbarities, so many and so various that to list each and every one of them individually would be the work of a lifetime.

I can vouch for the truth of the story that they made a practice of summoning caciques and other local leaders, ensuring them of their good will and offering them every assurance of safe conduct, and then seized them as soon as they appeared and burned them. In my presence they burned two such leading citizens, one in Ancón[131] and the other in Tumbes, and there was nothing I could do to stop them, even though I preached against it as effectively as I could. And, as God and my conscience are my witnesses, it was evident to all concerned that it was only because of this maltreatment that the peoples of Peru were finally provoked into revolt and took up arms against the Spanish, as, indeed, they had every cause to do.[132] For the Spanish never treated them squarely, never honoured any of the undertakings they gave, but rather set about destroying the entire territory, for no good reason and without any justification, and eventually the people decided that they would rather die fighting than put up any longer with what was being done to them.

I can further testify that local people have told me that there is a great deal more gold still hidden away than they have to date revealed, and that they have refused to hand it over to

131 Las Casas gives this as 'Andón'
132 This is a reference to the revolt of 1537–8 led by the Inca Tupac Amaru; see below, p. 115

the Spanish and will continue to refuse to do so for as long as they are unjustly treated in this cruel fashion, preferring, indeed, to take the secret to the grave, as have so many before them. The way the Spanish have behaved has been an offence to God and a disservice to the Crown; the Treasury has been defrauded and, in my opinion, it will be a long and a costly business to recover for the Crown this territory which could easily have provided sufficient food to support the entire population of Spain.

This, then, is the sworn testimony of Brother Marcos, and it has been witnessed and countersigned by the bishop of Mexico.

One has also to realize, when reading this testimony, that Brother Marcos was only talking of an area of some fifty to a hundred leagues in size and that all that he records happened nine or ten years ago, at a time when exploration of the region was in its infancy and only a handful of Spaniards were there. Since then, the siren call of gold has attracted four or five thousand Spaniards and they have explored vast tracts of territory, five to seven hundred leagues in extent, all of which they have plundered and all of which have witnessed acts of barbaric ferocity of the kind described and worse. And, since Brother Marcos's time, over a thousand times as many local people have been murdered, their lands devastated and their property stolen; indeed, a substantial proportion of the human race has been wiped out by these ruthless adventurers who fear neither God nor the King. The total death toll over these ten years in the region stands at more than four million souls, and the atrocities continue even today.

Only a few days ago they murdered a great queen, the wife of an Inca,[133] by impaling her on a number of bamboo shoots. Her husband[134] is the puppet king installed quite improperly by the

133 The text gives 'Elingue'
134 The reference would appear to be to the puppet ruler of Cuzco who led an unsuccessful revolt against the Spaniards in 1537–8

Spanish who had earlier seized him, and they murdered his wife in this fashion (and some say she was with child) quite without cause and simply in order to cause him grief.

If one were to set out in full each and every act of murder or cruelty committed by Christians in the kingdom of Peru, as well as those which are still being perpetrated today, they would doubtless make what we have described pale by comparison, so widespread and so dastardly are they.

THE KINGDOM OF NEW GRANADA

The year 1539 saw a number of adventurers set out from Venezuela, Santa Marta, and Cartagena for Peru. Others, already in Peru, set off inland to explore further. What they found, three hundred leagues inland from Santa Marta and Cartagena, was a vast fertile tract of beautiful country, home to a teeming population of people every bit as docile and virtuous as the natives of other parts of the New World, and extraordinarily rich both in gold and in those precious stones known as emeralds. This land they dubbed the kingdom of New Granada, because the first adventurer to clap eyes on it hailed from Granada in Spain.[135] The names of the Spaniards who come from all over to 'explore' this region figure high on the roll of honour of master butchers and experts in the spilling of human blood. Those concerned were veterans of some of the earlier bloody campaigns in other parts of the New World which we have already described; yet their appalling record in this new kingdom was such as to put all their previous exploits in the shade, for they now proceeded to commit outrages of a truly fiendish nature and on a quite unprecedented scale.

I shall give a short account of only one or two of the numberless crimes perpetrated over the last three years (and there is no indication of any let-up in such activity even today). It so happened that the then governor, determined to preserve for himself a free hand in plundering and murdering throughout this kingdom, baulked attempts made by one of these adventurers to get his hands on a share of the spoils. The individual who

135 Jiménez de Quesada. Other pioneers in the area included Nikolaus Federmann and Sebastián de Benalcázar

found himself thwarted in this fashion reacted by gathering together a number of eye-witnesses and compiling an official report of what was going on. This report, listing atrocities, outrages and widespread murder, was then laid before the Council of the Indies where a copy of it is still held to this day.

The witnesses swear that the whole kingdom was at peace and that the people were happily attending to the Spaniards' every need, continually bringing them things to eat that they had grown for themselves, tilling the soil for them, building houses, and presenting them with gold, the precious stones known as emeralds, and everything else they possessed or could obtain. To realize their long-term purpose of seizing all the available gold, the Spaniards employed their usual strategy of apportioning among themselves (or *encommending*, as they have it) [136] the towns and their inhabitants − ordinary people and leaders − and then, as ever, treating them as common slaves. The man in overall command of the expedition seized the king of the whole territory for himself and held him prisoner for six or seven months, quite illicitly demanding more and more gold and emeralds from him. This king, one Bacatá, [137] was so terrified that, in his anxiety to free himself from the clutches of his tormentors, he consented to a demand that he fill an entire house with gold and hand it over; to this end, he sent his people off in a search for gold, and bit by bit they brought it to him along with many precious stones. But still the house was not filled and the Spaniards eventually declared that they would put him to death for breaking his promise. The commander suggested they should bring the case before him, as a representative of the law, and when they did so, entering formal accusations against the king, he sentenced him to torture should he persist in not honouring the bargain. They tortured him with the strappado, put burning tallow on his belly, pinned both his legs to poles with iron hoops and his neck

136 See Introduction, p. xx
137 Las Casas gives his name as 'Bogotá'

They tortured him with the strappado, put burning tallow on his belly, pinned both his legs and his neck in iron hoops and burned the soles of his feet.

with another and then, with two men holding his hands, proceeded to burn the soles of his feet. From time to time, the commander would look in and repeat that they would torture him to death slowly unless he produced more gold, and this is what they did, the king eventually succumbing to the agonies they inflicted on him. The Lord sent a sign of His own abomination of such barbarity by burning down the entire town as they were in the very act of applying the torture.

Each of the other Spaniards in turn, versed as they were in nothing save the science of tearing hapless victims limb from limb, imitated his fine commander by devising fresh tortures for the cacique and lord of the town under his jurisdiction, even though these leaders and all their people had done nothing but minister to the Spaniards' every need and bring them more and more gold and emeralds. Such gifts were repaid by the donors' being tortured and having demands made of them for yet more gold and precious stones, and in this fashion the lords of the entire region were burned and dismembered.

A local lord, by name Daitama, was so terrified of the reputation for outrageous cruelty enjoyed by one such Spaniard that he took to the mountains along with his people in an attempt to escape such inhumanity. The local people see the mountains as a refuge and flight as a solution to their plight (though it is seldom an effective one); the Spanish term such action an 'uprising' and a 'rebellion'. When the villainous commander-in-chief heard what had happened, he sent reinforcements to help the very butcher whose ferocity had driven the peaceful and long-suffering natives to flee. They eventually tracked them down (for even in the bowels of the earth these people are not safe from the Spanish), and proceeded to hack to pieces over five hundred souls – men, women and children – slaughtering all and sparing none. Eye-witnesses record that, before the massacre, the local lord, this Daitama, presented his Spanish tormentor with four or five thousand *castilians*, but they killed him and massacred his people all the same.

The commander-in-chief arrived one night in another city where a large number of local people had offered their services to the Spaniards and had, with their customary humility and simple innocence, been ministering to their every need. Thinking it a good idea to do something that would terrorize the entire territory, he ordered his men to put the entire local population to the sword as they slept or ate their evening meal or rested from the day's labours.

In a separate incident, four or five hundred souls perished when the commander carried out a census to ascertain the numbers of caciques, lords and common people each Spaniard had as part of his household, and then ordered them all to be paraded in the square where he had them beheaded. According to witnesses, his notion was that this measure would cow the entire territory into submission.

There are eye-witness reports that another of these Spanish despots was the author of countless acts of cruelty, killing many people, cutting hands and noses off both men and women, and destroying whole communities.

On yet another occasion, the commander-in-chief posted to the province of Bogotá the officer who committed the atrocities just described, along with a number of other Spaniards, to investigate the question of who had succeeded to the throne now that he had tortured the old lord to death. They travelled many leagues, seizing every native they could. Because none was forthcoming about the identity of the heir to the throne, he cut the hands off some; others, women as well as men, he threw to wild dogs who tore them to pieces, and in these and like ways he butchered a great number of the natives. One day, just before dawn, he and his men fell upon a group of locals who were completely undefended because of solemn undertakings that they would not be attacked; indeed, the group, which included a number of the leaders who are known as caciques, had come down out of the mountains on the strength of the undertakings that had been given and had settled once again on the plain. Unprepared and unarmed, they were at the mercy of the attackers who took many men and women prisoners and, ordering them to lie flat on the ground with their arms stretched out in front of them, went round with a cutlass chopping off their hands, informing them the while that this was punishment for not revealing the whereabouts of the heir to the throne.

In a separate incident, this same fiend had his men attack the local people because they would not give him the coffer full of gold which he demanded. The death-toll was huge, and countless others, men and women, had their hands and noses hacked off while yet others were thrown to wild dogs who tore them to pieces and devoured them.

In one province, the local people were so terrified of this heartless and brutal enemy, after they had seen three or four or their leaders burned to death, that they retreated to a rocky prominence which promised to provide a strong natural defence. According to eye-witness accounts, there must have been four of five thousand of them on the rock when this fiend ordered a notoriously bloodthirsty companion-in-arms – one who had already carved his name high among those of his fellows on the roll of dishonour – with a small force to, as he put it, 'punish' these people for their 'rebellion'. Yet this was a 'rebellion' against the forces of plague and carnage, and it is the grossest distortion of the truth to suggest that the people themselves had done anything to deserve such 'punishment', or that the Spanish were in any sense the injured party; for it was the Spanish, not the local people, who should, in all justice, have been tortured without mercy, and yet it was they who now sought to inflict torture mercilessly on those they had offended. On the rock, the people stood, naked and unarmed; the Spaniards cried out that they only sought a peaceful end to the crisis and that, should the people cease to struggle, they would come to no harm. The people stopped fighting, the Spaniards rushed the rock, captured the strongholds, and then set about them. Like ravening lions and tigers, they tore into these docile sheep, slaughtering to left and to right and ripping bellies wide open with their swords. So many were there for them to hack to pieces that they had to call a break in order to rest, and after a short respite the captain ordered them to throw the survivors from the top of the rock which was indeed very high. This they did, and witnesses claim that the sky was quite darkened with the sheer numbers of falling bodies, some seven hundred of these poor wretches being dashed to pieces on the rocks below.

And, to put the finishing touches to this barbaric day's work, the Spaniards then conducted a thorough search for survivors hiding in the scrub, and the captain gave orders that any who were found were to be stabbed to death, which they were, and their bodies flung down on to the rocks. Even this consummate cruelty did not satisfy him, craving, as he did, yet more notoriety, and wishing to add to the enormity of his crimes; and so he gave orders for his men to herd the natives, men and women, they had taken alive (for, as in every such outrage, the men had taken a number of prisoners for themselves, including women and young boys) into a building made of straw, reserving only the very best for himself, and then set it on fire. Some forty or fifty perished in the flames and yet others were thrown to wild dogs who tore them to pieces and devoured them.

It was this same brute who was responsible for the deaths of some fifteen to twenty leading citizens in a town called Cota. He had them thrown to wild dogs who ripped them to pieces, and, while there, he also took many prisoners from among the local people, hacking off the noses of several women and children and the hands off many men and women. These (and there must have been some seventy pairs of hands in all) he eventually had strung up on a pole as a grisly warning to the rest of the town.

No pen can begin to do justice to the boundless cruelty of this enemy of God: he has been behind atrocities of a quite unprecedented brutality throughout the territory as well as in Guatemala province and, indeed, wherever he has journeyed in the New World (and it is now many years since he began the campaign of terror which has ravaged the region and completely destroyed its people).

The deposition which we have cited also contains testimony to the effect that the entire kingdom of New Granada has been so devastated by the barbarity of those in command and the wholesale slaughter, conducted either directly by them or with their tacit permission by those butchers and enemies of humanity who are their companions-in-arms (and the murders and cruelty continue unabated to this day), that there is every danger that, unless His Majesty takes steps in the very near future to put a stop to the killing of local people in order to extract gold from them, when they have already handed over all the gold they possess, there will soon be no native people left to work the land and the whole area will become one vast empty desert.

We can see, therefore, just how the pestilential tyranny of these cruel wretches has, in the two or three years since this kingdom was discovered, utterly transformed what was, according to all those who have been there and seen it for themselves, as well as according to the signatories to this deposition, the most populous region on the face of the earth, into a wilderness where respect for God and for the King are unknown. The carnage has been so brutal and on such a scale that those who are in a position to know can assert that unless His Majesty puts a stop to these hellhounds as quickly as may be there will be not a soul left alive throughout the territory. This is a view I endorse, having seen for myself just how these brutes can, in a very short space of time, devastate vast and prosperous areas and slaughter all who live in them.

There are two other great provinces, Popayán and Cali, which border on New Granada, as well as three or four more that are over five hundred leagues in size. These have all been ravaged and ruined in the same ways as those we have described, with the Spanish pillaging and plundering, murdering and torturing, and inflicting the same atrocities on the teeming population here as elsewhere in the region. The land is extremely fertile and beautiful and those who have returned recently from the region are full of the pain and sorrow which any visitor to the area must feel at seeing so many great towns and cities burned to the ground. In some one is faced with the sorry spectacle of fewer than fifty people scrabbling among the remains of what was once a town of a thousand or two thousand people, whilst other settlements are now totally ruined and abandoned. And there are areas, once teeming with people, where the only sight for a hundred leagues, or even two or three hundred, is of scorched earth and the blackened ruins of towns and cities. And, along the routes taken by these blackguards – from Peru, through the province of Quito and into New Granada, Popayán and Cali; via Cartagena and Urabá; from Cartagena to Quito; or along the San Juan river which runs parallel to the Pacific coast (and all these routes do eventually join up) – the indigenous peoples have simply been wiped out over a distance of six hundred leagues and more. The poor souls have been despatched to everlasting Hell and today the same fate is meted out to the innocent wretches who survive.

And, as if further proof were needed of the principle we enunciated at the beginning[138] that the longer these crimes of violence committed by the Spanish against these docile lambs reign unchecked, the crueller, more wicked and more inhuman they become, I can adduce the following examples of what is today happening in the region, examples of crimes that truly merit the everlasting torments of Hell-fire.

After the initial carnage and mayhem of conquest the Span-iards, as we have indicated, invariably subject the indigenous peoples to the horrors of slavery we have depicted; to one blackguard will fall two hundred natives, to another three hun-dred. The strategy favoured by the fiend in human shape in overall command of the territory is to parade a hundred of these poor wretches (and they answer his summons like lambs to the slaughter) and then to have thirty or forty of them beheaded on the spot, while he warns the others: 'I shall do the same to you if you do not obey my commands to the letter or if you try to run away.'

The reader may ask himself if this is not cruelty and injustice of a kind so terrible that it beggars the imagination, and whether these poor people would not fare far better if they were entrusted to the devils in Hell than they do at the hands of the devils of the New World who masquerade as Christians.

Another report makes me wonder which would carry off the

138 See above, p. 25

trophy as the finest example of cruelty, wickedness and untamed ferocity: the incident which we have just described or what I shall now mention. It has already been stated that in the New World the Spaniards have a number of wild and ferocious dogs which they have trained especially to kill the people and tear them to bits. It is not difficult to discover who are the real Christians and who are not when one learns that, to feed these dogs, they ensure that wherever they travel they always have a ready supply of natives, chained and herded like so many calves on the hoof. These they kill and butcher as the need arises. Indeed, they run a kind of human abattoir or flesh market, where a dog-owner can casually ask, not for a quarter of pork or mutton, but for 'a quarter of one of those likely lads over there for my dog', and undertake to repay the debt when he has 'killed another blackguard for myself'. Others take their dogs out hunting of a morning and, when they get back at lunch-time, answer questions about the morning's bag with a cheerful: 'Pretty good, actually. The dogs have accounted for fifteen or twenty of the blighters.' All of this you will find in recorded evidence given in the course of legal actions brought by one Spaniard against another. Is it possible to imagine anything more dreadful, more brutal, or more inhuman?

I should like now to say no more – until, that is, fresh reports arrive of worse evils (if such there could be) or until I am in a position to return to the region to see matters for myself. For forty-two years [139] now, these matters have been constantly before my eyes and on my mind, and I can honestly say, as God is my witness, that I have solid grounds for believing that the depredations, the harm, the destruction, the depopulation, the atrocities and massacres, the horrible cruelty and barbarism, the violence, the injustice, the plunder and the wholesale murder that all these territories have witnessed and their people suffered (and still suffer) are on such a scale that what I have here been able to

139 Las Casas did not in fact arrive in the Antilles until 1502

relate is no more than a thousandth part of the reality of what has been taking place and continues to take place.

Recognition of the truth will make the reader more compassionate towards the sufferings and the predicament of these poor innocent peoples and oblige him to adopt an even more stern and censorious attitude towards the abominable greed, ambition and brutality of their Spanish oppressors; and no Christian who reads this should be in any doubt, even for a moment, that there has ever been a single instance, from the date of the discovery of the New World down to the present, when the indigenous people have committed even the slightest offence against the Europeans without due provocation, and that it has been the wicked plunder and the treachery of the Europeans that have given rise to all the evils we have described. Indeed, the natives believed the Europeans immortal and to be descended from the heavens and they welcomed them as such, at least until the actions of these celestial beings finally revealed what sort of creatures they were and what it was they were after.

There is one other factor which merits a mention and it is that, from the very outset, the Spanish have taken no more trouble to preach the Christian faith to these peoples than if they had been dealing with dogs or other animals. Indeed, they have done their level best to prevent missionaries from preaching, presumably because they felt that the spread of the Gospel would in some way stand between them and the gold and wealth they craved. Today, the peoples of the New World are as ignorant of God as they were a hundred years ago: they have no idea of whether He is made of wood, or of air, or of earth. The only place where the missionaries have enjoyed a modicum of success is New Spain, but we are talking here of a very small corner of the New World and, for the most part, the local people have died and still die in the blackest ignorance of the faith and without the benefit of the Sacraments.

[CONCLUSION]

I, Bartolomé de Las Casas, or Casaus, a brother in the Dominican Order, was, by the grace of God, persuaded by a number of people here at the Spanish court, out of their concern for the Christian faith and their compassion towards the afflictions and calamities that befall their fellow-men, to write the work you have before you in order to help ensure that the teeming millions in the New World, for whose sins Christ gave His life, do not continue to die in ignorance, but rather are brought to knowledge of God and thereby saved. My deep love of Castile has also been a spur, for I do not wish to see my country destroyed as a divine punishment for sins against the honour of God and the True Faith. It had always been my intention to pen this account, although it has been long delayed by my being taken up with so many other tasks. I completed it in Valencia on the eighth day of December 1542, at a time when the violence, the oppression, the despotism, the killing, the plunder, the depopulation, the outrages, the agonies and the calamities we have described were at their height throughout the New World wherever Christians have set foot. It may be that some areas are worse than others: Mexico City and the surrounding territories are a little better than most, for there, at least, outrages cannot be committed so publicly, as there is justice of a sort, despite the crippling taxation unjustly imposed on the people. Yet I do see hope for the future, for, as the Emperor and King of Spain, Charles V (whose person and whose Empire may God preserve), learns of the crimes committed against his will and against that of God by his servants in the New World and of their treachery towards the people of the continent (for, until now, there has been an effective conspiracy of silence about what has really been happening), he will, as one wedded to the concept of justice and avid to see it prevail, put a stop to the wickedness and undertake a total reform of the administration of this New World that God has bestowed upon him and will do so for the greater glory of the Holy Catholic Church and for the salvation of his own royal soul. Amen.

After the above was written, a number of laws and ordinances, drawn up by His Majesty during a stay in Barcelona in November 1542, were given the royal assent and published in Madrid the following year.[140] These provide, in the most efficacious manner the drafters have been able to devise, for the eradication of the evil and godless crimes perpetrated against Our Lord and our fellow-human beings – crimes that threaten to bring a collapse of civilization and to presage the end of the world. His Majesty drew up the ordinances only after lengthy consultation with men of great learning and high moral standing, and after the issues involved had been fully debated in Valladolid. They were also approved in writing by true Christians, not only expert in theology but also completely free from the taint of the corruption and filth that has been indissolubly associated with the pursuit of wealth in the New World, the authorities there having been contaminated, body and soul, by the actions of those under them, a fact which goes a long way to explain why their agents have got away with destroying the region unchecked. Once the laws had been promulgated, those who, back at the Spanish court, were the prime movers behind the adventurism and the tyranny that has bedevilled the New World lost heart, because it seemed to them that the doors opening on to opportunity, exploitation and despotism had been shut in their faces. Many of them had copies of the New Laws made and sent them to various parts of the New World; and their agents on the ground (whose brief it was to plunder, exploit and devastate, and who had never known any regulatory check on their activities but

---

140 These are the famous 'New Laws'; see Introduction, p. xxvii

had rather revelled in a chaos worthy of Lucifer himself) saw, from the copies they had been sent, just what was in the New Laws. They were also informed by those in Spain on whose connivance they had always depended that they would have to observe these new dispensations; and when fresh and uncorrupt officials, charged with putting the new legislation into effect, arrived in the area, these godless agents, by now beyond any respect for the law, quite openly flouted the new provisions and, accepting that they had in effect placed themselves beyond the pale, proceeded to behave, particularly in Peru, as true outlaws, recognizing no limit whatever to their actions and inflicting a tyrannical misery on the people. Now, in 1546, Peru daily witnesses acts of a spine-chilling barbarity unequalled by any-thing seen before, either in the New World or anywhere else on earth, the upshot being that not only have entire indigenous populations been wiped out and their kingdoms abandoned, but God has decided to give them these butchers just deserts (the legal representatives of the Crown having proved ineffective against them) by turning them against each other. Many have died at the hands of their fellow-criminals.[141] In the wake of their open rebellion against the Crown, others, too, in many parts of the New World, have taken the law into their own hands and, while affecting to observe the new dispensations, are now in fact in open revolt. They have all been, in every case, extremely reluctant to give up the position and the wealth they have won for themselves during their lives of crime, and unwill-ing, also, to free the natives they have acquired and condemned to perpetual slavery. Now they have sheathed their swords and no longer murder the natives on sight, they have got into the habit of killing them slowly with hard labour and the imposition of other intolerable and totally unmerited vexations. And, to

141 The reference is to the civil war between the followers of the Pizarro brothers and those of one of Pizarro's former captains, Diego de Almagro. It lasted from 1537 until 1548 and nearly destroyed the colony

date, the Crown has not shown itself strong enough to put a stop to these injustices, because everyone, young and old alike, who journeys to the New World is either openly or in secret a fortune-hunter, albeit that some are worse than others, and all such fortunes are made at the expense of the local people. That they serve their own ends while pretending to serve those of the Crown is something that not only damages the Spanish interest but also brings dishonour on the name of God and on that of the King.

INDEX

THE STORY OF PENGUIN CLASSICS

Before 1946 ...'Classics' are mainly the domain of academics and students, without readable editions for everyone else. This all changes when a little-known classicist, E. V. Rieu, presents Penguin founder Allen Lane with the translation of Homer's *Odyssey* that he has been working on and reading to his wife Nelly in his spare time.

1946 *The Odyssey* becomes the first Penguin Classic published, and promptly sells three million copies. Suddenly, classic books are no longer for the privileged few.

1950s Rieu, now series editor, turns to professional writers for the best modern, readable translations, including Dorothy L. Sayers's *Inferno* and Robert Graves's *The Twelve Caesars*, which revives the salacious original.

1960s The Classics are given the distinctive black jackets that have remained a constant throughout the series's various looks. Rieu retires in 1964, hailing the Penguin Classics list as 'the greatest educative force of the 20th century'.

1970s A new generation of translators arrives to swell the Penguin Classics ranks, and the list grows to encompass more philosophy, religion, science, history and politics.

1980s The Penguin American Library joins the Classics stable, with titles such as *The Last of the Mohicans* safeguarded. Penguin Classics now offers the most comprehensive library of world literature available.

1990s The launch of Penguin Audiobooks brings the classics to a listening audience for the first time, and in 1999 the launch of the Penguin Classics website takes them online to a larger global readership than ever before.

The 21st Century Penguin Classics are rejacketed for the first time in nearly twenty years. This world famous series now consists of more than 1300 titles, making the widest range of the best books ever written available to millions – and constantly redefining the meaning of what makes a 'classic'.

The Odyssey continues ...

The best books ever written

PENGUIN (🐧) CLASSICS

SINCE 1946

Find out more at www.penguinclassics.com